AMERICAN VICTORY

AMERICAN VICTORY

Wrestling, Dreams, and a Journey Toward Home

HENRY CEJUDO
with Bill Plaschke

A CELEBRA BOOK

CELEBRA
Published by New American Library, a division of
Penguin Group (USA) Inc., 375 Hudson Street,
New York, New York 10014, USA
Penguin Group (Canada), 90 Eglinton Avenue East, Suite 700, Toronto,
Ontario M4P 2Y3, Canada (a division of Pearson Penguin Canada Inc.)
Penguin Books Ltd., 80 Strand, London WC2R 0RL, England
Penguin Ireland, 25 St. Stephen's Green, Dublin 2,
Ireland (a division of Penguin Books Ltd.)
Penguin Group (Australia), 250 Camberwell Road, Camberwell, Victoria 3124,
Australia (a division of Pearson Australia Group Pty. Ltd.)
Penguin Books India Pvt. Ltd., 11 Community Centre, Panchsheel Park,
New Delhi - 110 017, India
Penguin Group (NZ), 67 Apollo Drive, Rosedale, North Shore 0632,
New Zealand (a division of Pearson New Zealand Ltd.)
Penguin Books (South Africa) (Pty.) Ltd., 24 Sturdee Avenue,
Rosebank, Johannesburg 2196, South Africa

Penguin Books Ltd., Registered Offices:
80 Strand, London WC2R 0RL, England

First published by Celebra,
a division of Penguin Group (USA) Inc.

First Printing, January 2010
10 9 8 7 6 5 4 3 2 1

CELEBRA and logo are trademarks of Penguin Group (USA) Inc.

Library of Congress Cataloging-in-Publication Data:
Cejudo, Henry.
American victory: wrestling, dreams, and a journey toward home/Henry Cejudo with Bill Plaschke.
p. cm.
ISBN 978-0-451-22855-0
1. Cejudo, Henry. 2. Wrestlers—United States—Biography. I. Plaschke, Bill. II. Title.
GV1196.C45C45 2010
796.812092—dc22   2009029554
[B]

Set in Scala
Designed by Ginger Legato

Penguin is committed to publishing works of quality and integrity. In that spirit, we are proud to offer this book to our readers; however the story, the experiences, and the words are the author's alone.

*For those who believed in me and also those who
kicked me while I was down.
And most of all, for the U.S. of A. for being the
greatest country on earth, and whose outstretched arms gave
life to my family and fulfillment to my dreams.—H.C.*

*For Jennifer, whose faith gave me courage, whose
vision gave me strength.—B.P.*

AMERICAN VICTORY

★ ONE ★

The two fat dudes with leering grins and neck tattoos are leaning against a wall of my apartment complex, staring out at the dirt courtyard, watching a bunch of screeching kids play soccer.

It is downtown Phoenix, early summer, 1998, and nearly triple-digit degrees. I am not wearing a shirt, and there's sweat running down my chest. My hand-me-down cutoff jean shorts hang low off of my butt, revealing a pair of torn boxer shorts which used to belong to one of my older, bigger brothers. My tennis shoes are a size too big, so I wear thick white socks.

I'm not a great soccer player. But for some reason, I'm faster than most of these kids. And for every reason, I think I have more fire.

When the ball goes into the corner, some Mohawk-wearing punk from one of the downstairs units chases it down. And so I chase him down and run him over, flattening him and his creepy mesh gym shorts and his fancy Target tennis shoes. The ball rolls over into the corner, resting at the cowboy boot of one of the two men, who stops and catches it with his toe. I hustle over and lean down to pick up the ball, and that's when the man takes the toe of his boot and sticks it into my chest. I look up at his face, and there is a ragged scar running down the right side, into his greasy bearded stubble. His buddy has bushy eyebrows and smiles with some gold pieces where there should be teeth.

"Hey, boy," says the scarred man.

"Hey what?" I say.

"You like to fight?" he asks.

Do I like to fight? I don't know. I'm always fighting at home with my three brothers, but only because they are part of a family that overwhelms me, because I'm the youngest of six children forever crammed into a one-bedroom apartment where there's not even room for my own pillow. I'll fight my brothers for the remote control on the three-channel TV, or I'll fight my brothers for the last clean towel, so, yeah, I guess I fight at home. And sure, I also fight at school—kids who call me a midget because I'm short for my age, kids who call me dumb, nobody knowing how hard it is to spend six hours in quiet and controlled conformity when you come from chaos. Screw them.

"Yeah, I like to fight," I say.

"You wanna fight for money?" asks the gold-toothed man.

"Money?" I say.

"Fifty cents, enough to buy you a Mexican ice cream. How would you like that, kid?" he says.

I ask him what I would have to do. "Those kids you're playing with, those soccer kids, we'll match you up, pay you," he says.

"You gonna pay me to fight?" I say.

"To win," he says.

Later that afternoon, I am back in that dirt pile in the courtyard, only now all my friends are gathered around me in a circle, Target Shoes is standing across from me with his fists raised, and the two men are sitting in rusty lawn chairs, rubbing coins between their fingers.

My name is Henry Cejudo. I am eleven years old, and I am learning how to wrestle in a human cockfight.

Breathe. Please. Breathe.

Stop. Breathe. Hurting.

My mind wanders back from my dusty past to my steamy present, ten years and a zillion miles to a boiling room in the middle of the hottest spot on the planet right now, a sauna in the middle of a sauna at the end of August.

It is Beijing, China, the summer of 2008, and I'm a U.S. wrestler entered in the Olympics.

No shit.

I am the only twenty-one-year-old in a sport of guys who are all at least six years older. I'm ranked thirty-first in the world in a sport where only the top handful of guys ever win any medals or championships. I somehow won the Olympic Trials by beating a guy, Stephen Abas, who won a silver medal four years ago in the summer games in Athens. Someone who should be totally out of my league.

But somehow, I've made it; I have come to wrestling heaven, where I feel like I don't have a chance in hell.

Especially not since, at this moment, at noon on an August

afternoon in Beijing, in order for me to even compete in my weight division and have a chance at the medal, I have three hours to lose an absurd ten pounds. You heard that right. Three hours, ten pounds. Top that, Oprah.

You know about wrestlers cutting weight? At that moment, I had to not just cut weight, but amputate weight. I was supposed to weigh in 121.4 pounds, but I had suddenly somehow ballooned to at least 131 pounds. The weigh-in was in three short hours. If I was just one ounce over, my Olympic dream would be lost in lard and I would be too heavy to compete. Three hours, ten pounds. Eat that, Jared.

There are many ways that wrestlers cut weight. Sometimes they starve. Sometimes they spit and spit until they lose a bit of water weight. But when it comes down to the final hours and you still have a bunch of weight to get rid of, there is only one real way to do it, and that's to sweat. Lose all the water weight out through my pores.

When I awoke that morning, one day before my event, I wasn't worried about this too much. Sure, I was a young guy who was still growing, which adds weight. And maybe I ballooned a bit on the flight over from the United States, where the big wrestling star sat in coach, in the middle seat. And then there was the chance that even though I ate only fruit and chicken and drank only water while I had been in China, maybe I had eaten too much out of nervousness. Still, I was a little guy and I assumed nothing could screw me now that I was actually here, in China. But then I stepped on the scale in the wrestling room around noon and—damn! I nearly collapsed in fear. My coaches and brother and trainer shook their heads in frustration and confusion. Losing ten pounds in three hours was nearly impossible. Time for the heat. Time for the hurt.

Somebody went into the sauna and turned it on and up to 180 degrees. I stripped down to my boxer briefs and stepped inside. My handlers stepped in beside me carrying bottles of lotion. For the next thirty minutes, they slapped that lotion on my arms and legs—*slap, slap, slap*—trying to moisturize the perspiration out of me.

Did you know that 65 percent of the body is water? That's a lot of weight that can be sweated out of a dude. But did you also know that doctors recommend against anyone trying to cut more than five percent of their body weight? I'm sure they would recommend against the amputation that we were about to do.

I was trying to cut nearly 10 percent of my weight all at once. One day before competing in the Olympics. In a sauna in my underwear with my muscles being pounded by a bunch of guys covered in lotion.

My name is Henry Cejudo, and before being reborn as an Olympian, I had to die a slow death in the sauna.

Me against Target Shoes. My first fight. It felt so unfair. But it felt so good. Eleven years old and all grown up.

Standing in that dusty courtyard with the fat drunks waving their coins, I looked at Target Shoes and felt a momentary pang of pity. He was wearing nicer clothes than I was, sure, but that also meant he had softer eyes, a rounder belly, and knees that knocked. He was scared and had more to lose, and I felt sorry for him.

Until I threw his fat ass into the dirt. The drunks roared. The other kids howled. The roaches scurried at their feet—they didn't care about the fight except that we were disturbing them from infesting our apartments. The dust from the courtyard crept into my mouth. The kid stared up at me with fear as I held him down. Then he closed his eyes because he couldn't look. Bam. Bam. Bam. Bam.

I knew I was filled with fight. I had no idea I was also filled with anger. I couldn't stop myself, hitting this kid who looked like the son of every rich, fat landlord who had thrown us out of our apartments, pounding this kid who looked like the younger brother of every immigration cop who had given my parents a second look. Bam. This is for every night I went hungry. Bam. This is because I still don't have my own bed. Bam. This is for all the time you ran to your daddy, and I couldn't find mine.

After a few seconds, I leaned down into his trembling ear and whispered to him what I would eventually whisper to many of the people I would fight against in the future.

"Please quit," I said. "Quit before I kill you."

He rolled over into the fetal position as I felt two giant ringed hands picking me up into the air. It was one of the drunks. For winning, I had just won my prize of fifty cents for fried ice cream, and by betting on me, he had just won a couple of bucks for malt liquor.

I ran outside to find a vendor for the ice cream. I paid my money, a man finally, a little man with a big ice cream, and I tilted back my head and let it slide down my throat when I heard a familiar drunken call.

"Hey, boy!" said one of the fat guys. "We got more!"

More what? More money? More ice cream?

"More victims," he said, laughing in a tone that I despised, but smiling with a need that I needed too.

My name is Henry Cejudo, and before I was an Olympian, I kicked ass for drunks and dessert.

Not the clothes. Dear God. Not the clothes. Oh shit. Ouch. Oh no.

Back from the past again, my mind is focused on the sauna, where I have been baking for thirty minutes in my underwear in an attempt to lose ten pounds in three hours, where the horror is just beginning.

Now that I'm just starting to sweat, it's time to get dressed. In here. In layers. Like I'm in Minnesota in the middle of the winter instead of Asia in the summer.

First I put on a set of plastic pants and top, which immediately start burning my skin. Over that, I put on regular pants and a sweater. Then I lean down and put on thick socks. Then heavy shoes. Then a beanie hat. Everything is put on slowly so I can sweat while I'm putting it on. The overall effect is that of taking a nice stroll across the face of the sun.

I would say I was sweating like a pig, but I've never seen a weird neighbor's pet pig sweat like this. I felt like I was being beaten up under a hot shower. I felt like I was being boiled in a shallow saucepan. Every part of my body burned. Every muscle in my body soon began cramping.

I know this was unhealthy. I know that even if America's most devoted Olympic fans saw this, they would scream abuse. They were right. It was abuse. But willing abuse. By being ten pounds overweight just three hours before weigh-in, I had abused my privilege as an Olympian. I was now paying the price. It was my fault. I would pay with my sweat. Cutting weight was always part of every tournament. I grew up doing it, so I knew what I was doing and I wasn't fighting it. But it doesn't mean it wasn't painful, and it doesn't mean that the crushing weight of an upcoming Olympic tournament didn't make it unbearable.

After an hour in the sauna, my handlers pushed me outside the room and into a hot courtyard, where they plopped me on a bike. Still wearing the plastic underwear. Still wearing the sweaters. Still wearing the damn beanie.

"Pedal," shouted Angel, my brother and wrestling partner.

"Screw you," I shouted back.

But of course I pedaled, as hard as I could, for forty-five minutes while wearing what felt like forty-five pounds of clothes. When I finally stumbled off the bike, somebody handed me a rope. I thought this might be a good time to hang myself with it. They wouldn't let me.

"Jump!" shouted Angel.

"Piss off," I shouted back.

But obviously, I jumped with the rope, skip, skip, shit, skip, jumping while covered in my own water, jumping as if I was leaping into the deep end of the pool, stopping every couple of minutes to see if my thumb and forefinger fit around my wrist. If they did, I knew, I would make weight. If they didn't, I wouldn't.

The fingers still didn't fit around my wrist. I kept jumping rope until I was actually more stumbling rope, then walking rope, barely getting my shoes around the rope as it slowly twirled over my head. I finally stopped and slumped in front of my coach, Terry Brands.

"I'm done, I'm done," I said.

"We'll see," he said, leading me over to an outdoor scale.

I stripped off my clothes. I stepped on the metal. One pound over. One hour until the weigh-in, I was exhausted and dehydrated and hallucinating, seeing myself as that little kid fighting in the dirt courtyard, seeing myself fighting for the fat drunks, seeing myself nearly dying at their feet. One pound over? How in the hell was I was going to lose that final pound?

For anyone strolling on the sidewalks outside the USA Wrestling wrestling rooms at Beijing Normal University on that pretty August afternoon, well, now you know.

That naked, shivering, screaming, weeping kid?

My name is Henry Cejudo, and that was me.

His mom was tough. I'd seen her skulking under the stairwells, smoking dope, and making threats. But I'd seen him hanging on the pockets of her jeans like a little baby.

She was tough. He was scared. But she was going to make him fight me anyway.

I don't remember the exact name of that boy who was shoved in front of me on one of those early-evening fights at the apartment complex. I only knew that, while he was a few inches taller than me, he was skinny, and slow, and had nothing of his mother's meanness in him. I also knew that I didn't give a shit about any of that, because I was hankering for some ice cream and for a fight and I would've taken on anyone.

I whacked him in the face and he fell. I dropped on top of him and grabbed his hair, banged his head on the dirt and he moaned.

"Enough! Enough!" shouted one of the laughing drunks, doing the usual drill of pulling me off the kid.

Only this time, the kid didn't get up and leave. He slowly stood, brushed himself off, and stared at me as his mother screeched in the background.

"Fight him again!" she shouted.

"Fight me again?" I wondered at her.

One of the drunks pulled out a wad of green money, handed it to another drunk, they both laughed, and soon they joined the mother in shouting at her beaten boy.

"Be a man; fight him again," they chimed.

He took two steps toward me. I shrugged and hit him in the chest, then slapped him in the head, then threw him back to the ground. He stared up at me with no anger, no fear, just numbness. I was pulled off his motionless body when I heard the cries again.

"One more time!" shouted his mother. Saying crazy stuff to her son like, "You get your ass off the ground and fight him again."

My mother wasn't around. She was probably walking the streets selling tamales, or she would have stopped it. My brothers were around, watching and howling, so there was no way they would have stopped it. That boy's only protection was his own people, and they were sending him back to the wolf, damn them.

The boy stood up, walked toward me like a robot, and it was only then that I noticed a trickle of blood coming from his mouth, and a tear coming from his eye.

Oddly, as I cocked my fist, I suddenly stepped outside myself. And, for the first time in my young life, I think I learned something about myself.

Because I didn't hit him. Instead, I clenched him. I held him tight and pushed him backward, his nervous sweat dripping on my shirt. I leaned over and whispered into his ear.

"They want me to kill you," I said. "Don't make me kill you. Fall down under me. Curl up. Act like you're knocked out. I'll go home and you'll survive."

His mom was standing behind him now, waving her arms and screaming for her boy to "get tough!" so he began to push back, and I squeezed him even harder.

"Fall down now!" I said. "Please, fall down, close your eyes, save yourself."

Thump. With a grand fall worthy of any great actor, the boy fell to the ground. This time I stood up myself, looked down, made sure his eyes were closed, and stalked away while he was surrounded by kids who thought he was dead. A couple of days later, of course, he was running with me in a soccer game, very much alive.

I truly believe I might have saved a life that day. Maybe two lives. Because maybe I also saved my own. I learned that while I could be consumed by anger, I also possessed this oddly deep sense of compassion. Having grown up poor and forgotten, I wanted to beat the happiness out of those who would never understand where I came from and how I suffered. But it turns out I also wanted to hug the happiness into those who did.

The son of the gangster lady, he understood.

My name is Henry Cejudo, and by the time I was twelve years old, I was already wrestling for my life, fighting for my soul.

———————

"Get your ass back in the sauna!"

My focus left the memories of that battered kid and centered again on this battered man, that being me. I was one pound over with less than an hour remaining. This was crisis time. Terry Brands, my coach, was screaming at my naked body as he shoved me back into the room from hell. My handlers followed him, and soon they were on me again like mosquitoes, pinching and rubbing the sweat out of my skin, so slow, so painful.

You know when you have a cramp in your leg? A day before the beginning of my official Olympic experience, I had a cramp in my entire body. I was twitching and screaming in fear and pain, but also with determination. One pound. One hour. Breathe. Breathe. Breathe.

I think I must have passed out at some point, because, after about ten minutes of being back in that sauna, suddenly everything went black, then incredibly light, then I was slumped on a scale and—thank you, pain—I made my weight. It was 121.4 pounds exactly. I had succeeded. I was cooked—literally—but I had lost the weight. The following day, I was finally, actually going to be able to compete in the 2008 Olympics.

I raised my arm in jubil—nah. I could barely move. I could barely walk twenty steps without being propped up. My handlers threw me in a tank of cold water. This is when, officially, even my lips and tongue cramped.

"At least this will shut you up," said Angel.

"Pftpftpft," I answered.

Thus I rode to my glorious weigh-in while curled up in the back of a car, still in agony. After arriving at the wrestling venue,

I lay on the floor in a back room because I was too weak to even stand in line.

But I was eventually able to climb up on the scales. No, I didn't gain any weight while swallowing the dirty air in the backseat of that car on the way to get weighed in. Yes, I was officially, finally, thankfully cleared to compete in the next day's Olympics.

You may know what happened then. You may have read how I defeated four of the top wrestlers in the world and reached the finals as America's youngest wrestling gold medalist ever and one of the most improbable potential gold medal winners in Olympic history and . . . well, I'm not going to give away the ending, at least not here. You'll have to keep reading.

The title of this book is *American Victory*. But if you know anything about my story, you know that it's about much more. It is a story not just of an American, but of a Mexican-American, born of parents who were illegal aliens, the father a drunk and drugged-out bum, the mother a strong and silent single parent. It is a story not just of a victory but of countless failures and humiliations along the way, the story of a child who grew up in junkyards and shacks from Los Angeles to Las Cruces to Phoenix.

It is a story of a child who found unlikely solace in the chaos of a wrestling mat, and an unlikely spot with the U.S. Olympic team. In the beginning, he wasn't even summoned to the Olympic Training Center in Colorado Springs to win a gold medal. He was summoned to serve as a practice wrestler for women wrestlers who were going to compete in the Athens Olympics.

He was low ranked, lightly regarded, a pain in the butt to his classmates, a cocky punk to his elders. A lucky break got him into the 2008 Summer Games, and a stupid weight miscalculation nearly disqualified him before he started. He trailed everyone he wrestled. He needed last-second saves to survive nearly every match. His mother wasn't there because she had no passport, and his father wasn't there because he had died far away and in great pain. The wrestler was alone and against all odds and, well, again, I don't want to tell you what happened.

American Victory?

My name is Henry Cejudo, and I want to take you on my journey that could just as easily have been called American Madness.

★ TWO ★

I remember bars. Giant black bars. Everywhere, bars.

I was born in a city of blue skies and sunshine, and what I remember most are the bars.

Viewed from my family's first apartment in South Central Los Angeles, where my parents settled after sneaking here from Mexico, the world was covered in black metal. I don't remember the cool breeze or the warm green grass. I remember the black bars covering the windows and front doors, black bars surrounding the playgrounds, black bars even twisted over soda and candy machines.

I grew up in a prison. That's how it looked. That's how it felt.

I was born on February 9, 1987, the youngest of six children of Nelly and Jorge Cejudo. They weren't supposed to be here. They didn't feel wanted here. They were Mexicans who had stolen across the border illegally, my father crouched in the back of a truck, my mother in high heels as she elegantly crossed a desert that was supposed to lead to paradise.

My mother thought she was going to Disneyland. Instead, she ended up in a life that spun her around like the teacups ride. My father thought he was going to be some kind of Aztec conqueror. Instead, he couldn't even defeat his own demons.

When I was born, I was the sixth of six children, two girls, four boys, all under the age of nine. The oldest was eight-year-old Barbara. Then there was Alonzo, who was two years younger and was six at the time; then came Gloria, who was four, Jorge who was two, Angel was one year old, and then there was me. Eight years later, my mother would give birth to my little sister, Christie, but for now, six was more than enough.

We lived in a one-bedroom hovel in the Southgate Apartments in South Central Los Angeles, a shoe box of a place that contained the biggest irony on the block. My father worked at a furniture store, yet we never had any furniture of our own. Eight people, and no beds, no couches—just giants piles of colorful blankets that we pushed against walls and underneath windows covered in those bars. We would sleep and eat and play in those blankets—they were our tables, our chairs, and our beds.

The furniture was gone, because my father was gone. At least, most of the time he was gone. When he was home, well, okay, I guess he was also pretty much gone then, too. He would walk into the house with booze reeking from the tattoos on his chest, with cigarette and marijuana smoke reeking from his stained wifebeater undershirt.

I would know he was home from the sight of his shoes. Not his shoes walking around on the floor, but the sight of them in the air. From my bedroom, I could see his black shoes flying

across the living room. I knew those shoes were aimed at my
mother, because then I would see her red shoes flying in the opposite direction right back at him. Black. Red. Black. Red. Like
some sort of sick game of airborne checkers, the shoes would fly
at each other as I hid, burrowed in those blankets. I could tell the
fighting would end only when I would hear those black shoes
slip on my father's feet, and my father stalk out the door. The red
shoes never went back on my mother's feet. She never left. She
always stayed. For my entire life, she stayed. She would hold me
when I cried for his absence, restrain me when I reached for his
ghost, comfort me when I longed for his presence. And never,
not once, did she say bad things about that man who was so
much trouble.

My father was trouble, but, man, I loved him. To me, he was
Superman. A drunken Superman.

He was hard to love because he did more than just ignore us
or avoid us. He wasn't just an absentee father. Life would have
been much easier if my father was actually absentee. The real
problems occurred when he showed up.

In my first Christmas memory, I'm four years old, wearing my
older brother's clothes, eating my older sister's leftovers, sleeping on blankets with no pillows, and suddenly there are flashing
lights filling our living room, and they weren't from the cars
outside on the street. It was a Christmas tree. It looked more like
a Christmas bush, something out of a Charlie Brown movie that
we had never watched back then because we didn't own a TV, but
something small and weak and freaking wonderful.

A Christmas tree. And underneath it, Christmas presents,

six little packages wrapped up in paper adorned with birthday cakes. It may have been the wrong kind of wrapping paper, but it was the right time of year, our first real Christmas presents. One for each of us. To this day, I don't know how my mom set up that tree. It was at night, when we were sleeping, and it just appeared out of nowhere. Also, to this day, I don't know where my mom got those presents. Maybe it was Goodwill, or church handouts, or neighbors who didn't need them anymore. I just know she would do anything to try to show that even our sad little home could be filled with magic. She was trying like hell to be our Santa Claus. She was doing her best to be a savior.

I remember everyone drawn to the little presents, hovering over the little boxes as if, inside, they contained some sort of magnets. I remember two of my brothers tumbling into the boxes while trying to keep each other away from them, their fight nearly tearing apart our Christmas. But the boxes survived. That night we all huddled expectantly in the other room, four boys on one bunch of red blankets, two girls and Mom on another bunch of green blankets, everyone eagerly waiting for the morning celebration.

Then we heard it. A creak of a window. The unhinging of a screen. A heavy thump, then a couple of light steps. I knew it. I just knew it. It was the real Santa. The closest thing we had to a fireplace was a bum's burning box outside on the curb. The nearest thing we had to a chimney was a nest of hungry rats that scurried around on the roof. But by God, we had a Christmas tree, so I knew we had the possibility of a visit from Santa Claus.

"Santa?" I whispered to my brothers, clutching their bare arms in excitement and fear.

"Santa," they whispered back in voices that contained traces of the same fear.

"Stop!" screamed my mother, leaping from her blanket and walking swiftly out of the bedroom toward the tree.

What? What was happening? Did my mother think Santa was a burglar? Was she going to attack him and ruin Christmas? No, no, no, she couldn't do that! I leaped to my feet in an attempt to catch the hem of her tattered white nightgown as she stalked into the living room and . . .

Shit. I didn't say it out loud. I probably didn't even say it right, but I clearly remember that this was the first moment in my life when I actually cursed.

Shit. As I could plainly see, our visitor was no Santa Claus. That was my father. That was Jorge Cejudo. He was dressed in baggy khakis with a rag hanging out the back and an old sweatshirt with the pits stained dark. I remember seeing his face, the twinkling of the Christmas lights reflecting off of it. This was not the kind face of someone who was giving. This was the hardened, beard-stubbled expression of someone who was taking.

Shit. Shit. Shit. My father was stealing our Christmas presents. He had them wrapped in his arms and was using his butt to open our door and carry them out into the street.

"Stop! Stop! Stop!" shouted my mother, chasing him into the cool night air as we heard his footsteps pattering down the block.

Moments later she returned with a look that I'll never forget. Her eyes were lined with a deep sadness, yet her mouth was forced into a crooked smile. It looked like she was biting her lips. It looked like her mouth was caught in some painful spasm that refused to let it frown. She was so hurt. Yet her face would not let her show it. My father stole our Christmas presents. He would not steal our Christmas.

"Everybody, back to bed, back to bed. Now you see that Santa Claus doesn't exist—he never did. We don't need him; we only need each other. Everybody, back to bed," she said in her native Spanish to the six children who had gathered by the tree still swaying from the weight of my father's crime.

And so, hours after I first believed in Christmas, I saw how you can never believe in Christmas. We never did find out what was in those boxes. And since then, whenever I hear Christmas carols on the radio of the discount stores where I still shop, I wince, for the most compelling holiday sounds in life will always be, not of bells and jingles, but of my mother, in the middle of that Christmas night, after believing that all of us children had fallen asleep, sobbing into those blankets.

The next day we awoke, dressed, attended church for the Christmas service, walked together to the park, stopped and bought sidewalk hamburgers for our Christmas dinner, then came home and rolled around playfully in front of that tree. Shortly after losing everything, it felt like we had lost nothing. Like it was okay we didn't have any presents. It was the beginning of a life lesson that my mother taught us with great pain, but with great pride. In this life, you make your own happiness. The world can steal everything you might own, all your possessions, but it cannot steal your spirit. In this life, you stand tall and walk steady and fight for that spirit.

That was, not coincidentally, the last time we had Christmas presents under the tree for several years. Instead of risking disappointment, we would line up for toys outside a discount store that was giving them away on Christmas Day. Of course, those toys came with their own kind of disappointment. We would wait all day, get a toy gun, come home, beat the crap out of it, break it in two hours, and that was that until next year. We would spend the rest of Christmas vacation playing with each other. We learned that possessions mean nothing as long as you've got your family.

Funny thing about my father. He came back home about a week after stealing our Christmas presents, and all of a sudden he was my father again. The older kids didn't want to be near him, but I couldn't stay away from him. I was the only one in the family with the innocence to still love him, the only one who still needed to believe in him, the youngest kid who still needed to look up to him, so we hung out together. He would call me "*Me Campion*"—my champion—and tell me that if I wanted to grow up strong, I needed to drink carrot juice. Imagine that. The first person to convince me I could be a champion was a loser, and the first person to teach me about training was a lazy drunk.

I didn't care. Superman, remember? He had already spent some time in prison for drinking and drugs, so he had those prison yard muscles and those prison tattoos, and I wanted to be like that. He was also the first person who made me want to be tough, especially when he was raining his abusive toughness on me.

The best example of that is carrot juice. Yeah, carrot juice. We could buy it cheaply down the street, or my father had some buddies who just gave it to him, but whatever, he really wanted me to drink carrot juice. He thought it would make me strong. And at first, I loved it. It was the one thing my father ever asked me to do for him, and I loved making him happy. But eventually, I came to hate carrot juice. I liked grape soda. I liked real fruit juice. Carrot juice was neither. It was gross. So one day, I took the carrot juice to the backyard where we had an empty and rusty junk refrigerator. By the way, it wasn't until I was an adult that I realized not everybody had an empty, rusty major appliance on their lawn. Ours was a refrigerator, and I walked back there with my carrot juice and tossed it onto the brown dirt behind that refrigerator. I smiled and turned to walk back in the house when I smelled the beer.

My father was standing right there. He had seen what I done. The next thing I felt was a hot hand on my head, swatting me into blackness. Then I felt another hand on the other side of my head, and one on my stomach, my father pummeling me into that carrot juice–covered dirt. I've been in thousands of fights in my life, but never have I been beaten like I was beaten that day.

Years later, before one of my big matches, my mentor, Tracy Greiff, had this bright idea of going to Costco and buying me some high-energy drink. "Henry, I've got a surprise for you. This will give you pep. You'll love it. You probably never thought of it," he told me.

"What is it?" I asked.

"Carrot juice!" he said.

I nearly leg whipped him on the spot.

Still, beyond all reason, I loved my father. I still felt like I was special to him. *"Me Campion."* He didn't say it to anyone else. He was just mean to everyone else. I remember once my brother Alonzo came to him suggesting that the family's old junk car be traded in for a convertible. "You want a convertible?" he said. "Here, I'll give you a convertible." And with that, my father walked outside with a power saw that he had "borrowed" from a neighbor and cut the top of the car, ruining it forever and blaming it on Alonzo. Yep, now my brother has his convertible.

While my father gave me my craziness, my mother gave me my comfort. She used to sing me to sleep, until she realized that the softness of her voice—a sudden change from my hardened world—made me cry. She would take me to church, clutching my hand in the pew, talking to me about my fear of the devil on the walk home past the neighborhood demons.

It was also my mother who first exposed me to wrestling. She didn't understand or enjoy the sport, and it would be years before she actually attended one of my matches, but when I was four years old, she took me and my older brother Angel to a dime store in South Central Los Angeles and bought us little professional wrestling action figures. She bought me Hulk Hogan. She bought my brother the Ultimate Warrior. And then when we got home, she laughed as we tried to imitate these figures, me tearing off my shirt, my brother ripping up his shirt, both of us running into each other in the cramped living space that passed for our apartment. She didn't stop us. She laughed with us, especially the time I came out of the bathroom wearing only my underwear and covered in baby oil.

"Who are you supposed to be?" my mother asked me, speaking only Spanish, just as she does today.

"I am a wrestling champion!" I shouted, as her laughter rose and her eyes twinkled.

I will never forget that laugh, or those eyes, or that giant smile on the Mother's Day that Angel, Jorge, and I came home with fresh roses for my mom. She had just set them up in a tin can in the corner when there was a knock on the door.

"Run!" I shouted, and my brothers and I clamored into the bathroom.

"Why are you running?" my mother asked before opening the door and discovering why.

Standing outside were two policemen.

"Ma'am, we have a report that some men in this house have been trespassing and stealing flowers from the neighbors," they said.

"Oh my," my mother said.

Locked up with my brothers in that bathroom, I heard that scared tone in my mother's voice and began to cry. I never wanted to hurt her. I only wanted to make her happy. My brothers tried to hold me back, but I broke free and stumbled back into the main room.

"I'm sorry. I'm sorry," I wailed.

My mother's smile returned, and she looked up at the cops and shook her head.

"Well, Officers, there's one of your dangerous men," she said.

The policemen left, and my mother walked over to smell the flowers, and I lay there on the floor looking up at the strongest woman I would ever meet.

I loved in a more unconditional manner. I loved my father even when he acted like he hated me. I remember once walking down a neighborhood street with my family when we came upon a garage sale. There was a familiar-looking toy on one of the tables. It was a Hulk Hogan action figure with a little chip in it. It looked exactly like one that I had, but lost. I begged my mother to buy it back for me, but she refused. Turns out, she knew something I didn't know and wouldn't understand for several years. My father had taken that action toy from me and sold it to the neighbor kids for a couple of bucks. He actually did that. I later learned that my father was an expert in borrowing things from neighbors, selling them to someone else, then "borrowing" them back. Like vacuum cleaners. He sold more vacuum cleaners than a Hoover man, only none of them were his.

Then there were the drugs. Talk about a master salesman. He moved all kinds of drugs, and sometimes turned our little houses into ganja dens. I remember once my mother asking my brother Alonzo and me to go outside and pick some mint from the yard for something she was cooking. Alonzo said, "We don't need to go outside; we have some in here." Then he grabbed me and pulled me into a back closet in the bedroom. There, on the floor, hidden under a bunch of old clothes, were giant black plastic bags. My brother happily dug inside one of them and produced giant handfuls of what he thought was mint.

"Mommy, come look!" he shouted.

My mother came back, saw the stuff in Alonzo's hands, and turned white.

"That's not mint!" she said.

It was marijuana. My father had stored enough dope in our closet to send him to prison for the rest of his life. Most of my family wished that he would get caught, so he could experience the sort of confinement that my family, being without money or education or any real hope, felt every day. And we didn't want him getting the rest of us in trouble. But me, I didn't want him to get caught. I wanted him to fly free forever. My drunk daddy Superman. When my father came home that day and was confronted with his crime, he hastily moved all the bags out of the house and toted them down the block. He was so embarrassed, he came back to the house and went through my mother's perfume drawer. At first I thought, Why is he acting like a woman? Why would he want perfume and to smell like a woman? Then he took the caps off the perfume and drank them. Oh, yeah, he was just acting like an alcoholic.

While my father was coming and going, so were we. We moved several times in my first five years, from apartments to garages to the backs of houses. We moved when we couldn't pay the rent. We moved when we tried to lose my father.

The only constant was the lack of food. Our steady diet was of beans and tortillas—and then hunger at the end of the month after the food stamps ran out. The best meals we had came from school. Free breakfast and lunch, nine months a year. Most kids longed for summer, but we hated it, because it meant we would spend the next three months hungry.

There really seemed to be no place for us. My mother had recently been granted permanent resident status as part of the immigration legislation of 1986, which provided amnesty to aliens who had been living here for a certain period of time. So she had her green card. But back then, there were fears within the Mexican-American community that the status could be revoked at any time. She couldn't leave the country, she couldn't bring anyone into the country, and she better behave while she was living in the country. So she still felt like she couldn't walk around without worrying that someone was going to throw her in a truck and drive her back to the border.

Anybody who asks how I have such great sight and perception on a wrestling mat, I tell them that it's because my mother had eyes in the back of her bun and I learned it from her. She never felt at home here, or completely at ease.

I also felt isolated at first, but for a different reason. Growing up in a Latino neighborhood, I was a funny sight, as I was born with fairly light skin and bright blond hair. Seriously. I guess it was a weird genetic thing. But it was also nearly tragic. Once my mother was walking me home from the park. I was wearing only a diaper and sandals. A police car roared up, and out jumped two cops. They looked at this dark Latina woman toting this white, blond child, and they drew only one conclusion. She had stolen me. There had actually been a report of a stolen child filed a couple of hours earlier, so they were convinced my mother was a kidnapper.

I wasn't old enough to remember what happened, but I was told that she was forced to sit on a park bench and answer an hour's worth of questions before they let her, and me, go. They couldn't deport her, but she was never sure about that, so she trembled as she held me and handled the questions. Some women might have caved under that fear, said anything to get released, and at least temporarily lose their child. My mother held firm, kept insisting that I belonged to her, and the cops finally relented.

Thank goodness. I did belong to somebody. Good or bad, I belonged to my family. We had no permanent home, but somehow, beneath all the crap, there beat a permanent heart.

We would share clothes. My sisters dressed like boys for many years because that's the only kind of clothes we had. I dressed in oversized pants and shirts because none of the hand-me-downs fit quite right. But if somebody made fun of us at school, all of us would run out to fight them. We stuck together.

We would share those blanket beds. That made us closer. When you grow up spending long hours with your brother's leg in your face and your sister's foot in your hand, you get to feel part of him and her.

We would share our food. Even today, I consider everything I order anywhere to be family style. I'll share with anybody, because, down to the last tortilla, we learned to cut it up and share with each other.

And, of course, we would share our pain. Would we ever. Even during some of my happier childhood moments, there was pain. But we had each other, and we felt like the only ones who knew what the other was going through.

I'll never forget my first cement circus. It was one of those traveling carnivals that sets up in deserted inner-city parking lots, one big creaky Ferris wheel, a bunch of rides that twirl in circles to the blaring tune of heavy metal music, a row of shooting and baseball-throwing games run by guys with fast hands and no teeth, and endless booths of greasy fried dough and stale cotton candy. In short, for a kid, it was paradise.

These carnivals were cheap, and my father had a few bucks in his pocket from who-knows-where, and he wanted to spend it on his "little *campion*" so we came, and it was wonderful, walking through clanging and ringing and whistling, my father both daring and protecting, his giant callused paw clutching my littlehand, sweat pouring off his arms in beer-scented rivulets. We stopped at a booth to throw baseballs at stuffed cats, and my father nearly beaned the greasy-haired worker instead, by accident. We stopped at another booth to shoot water into a clown's mouth; my father was finally teaching me how to attack life, how to find your aim, how to succeed, when . . .

"Jorge Cejudo?"

The voice was in English, the face behind it was white, and I knew he was in trouble. Growing up in South Central Los Angeles, I rarely saw any white people. And when I did, somebody was always getting handcuffed and carried away.

Shit. I said it for the second time in my life.

"Jorge Cejudo?"

I'll never forget how my father's hand left my hand and stuck straight into the air. I rushed into my mother's nearby arms and watched, my drunk Superman suddenly grounded, pulled back to earth and reality.

Yeah, it was the police. Yeah, they had finally caught up with my father. I don't know how they found him here, and I'm not sure exactly why he was nabbed, most likely drugs and theft, but to this day, I don't know, and I don't care. The only thing that mattered was, right in front of the squirt gun clowns, the cherry-colored elephant ears, a bunch of little girls squeezing their cotton candy, and me, my father was arrested at the fair.

"That's my father!" I shouted to one of the two cops as they loudly fastened the cuffs.

"*Me Campion!*" my father shouted back to me as he was slowly led away through trash-strewn asphalt.

Our voices could be heard above the blaring of some rock song that I do not remember, but will never forget.

"Daddy!" I shouted.

"I will be back!" he shouted.

It had, up until that point, been one of the greatest days of my life. Suddenly it became what turned out to be the single most prophetic and painful. Kids gathered around and gawked. Parents shook their heads and whispered. My mother's entire body slumped, as if every bone had just been removed. Then, just as quickly, she straightened up and grabbed my hand.

"Honey, let's buy some churros," my mother whispered, dragging me away as I turned and strained for a look at Superman's rippled, sweaty, hunched shoulders being led past the Tilt-A-Whirl.

I was five years old, and I would never see my father again.

★ THREE ★

"Sit here."

"Sit where?"

"Just sit here!"

Here was nowhere. Here was nothing. But here was my life, on a bench at a bus stop outside a creaky, run-down gas station on a sand-strewn, abandoned splotch of New Mexico.

We had just ridden on two separate cramped, sweltering, urine-reeking buses for nearly twenty-four hours, for a distance of about 770 miles, our world stuffed into cardboard boxes that we carried ourselves and our hopes smashed all to hell. Seven of us—Mom and six young kids—were traveling from Los Angeles to Las Cruces, New Mexico, to start a new life, or at least, to try and obliterate the idea of our old one for now.

Running from something? You bet. We were running from our father, who was scheduled to be released from jail that day after his carnival arrest resulted in six months in the slammer.

We were running from a threat that, unknown to us kids at the time, he had issued just days before his arrest.

"I'm going to shoot them all," he had screamed at my mother during a drunken rampage, waving his gun at our sleeping forms. "I'm going to shoot him, and him, and him, and her!"

"Wait!" my mother apparently shouted back in a desperate attempt at distraction. "Let me do it for you! I'll kill one, then you kill one, then I'll kill one."

My father was so confused and disoriented by this unexpected request that he stumbled from the house, back into the sort of trouble that eventually landed him in jail. My mother did not tell us about it at the time. Six months later, when the official-looking letter arrived warning us of his release, she knew he would be back, only this time she was worried that he might actually take her up on her offer. So she spilled her guts in the only way she ever spilled them to us.

"Pack your things; we're moving," she said, no explanation given, no explanation needed.

We were moving to Las Cruces, of all places, because one of our former church pastors lived there with his wife and six kids. It was one place where my mother knew someone. We were moving on this morning, of all mornings, because my mother had just gotten her welfare check. Enough to pay for bus fare and food for the journey.

Running from something, yes. Running to something? Hell no. We didn't know anything about Las Cruces. We had no idea when or even if we would get there. I was just five years old, but still I remember how we spent the better part of a day sitting on each other's laps and sweating through each other's clothes and trying not to puke all over each other's laps while riding on the bus.

When we arrived at the first bus station inside the Las Cruces city limits, my mother gathered us around an outside bench and told us to sit. We wondered why. We had just spent nearly a full day sitting. Where was the pastor's house? Where were his kids? Where were we going?

Turns out, my mother had no idea.

Turns out, she had packed all of our stuff without ever calling the pastor, and had crammed us onto this unsanitary bus without ever warning the pastor or his wife that we were coming. We had come to Las Cruces without being invited or expected or even wanted.

It was as if she didn't realize this fact until we were trudging off that bus and plopping down on that bench, dust blowing through our air, a poor Mexican family with its life summed up in the pile of junk at its feet.

"Mom, what are we going to do?" asked my sister Gloria.

"Just sit!" my mom shouted.

For four hours, while my mom fought with her pride, we sat. For four hours, while my mom worked up the courage to make the call for help, we sat.

We were hungry, so she bought us potato chips and soda from the gas station. She walked back inside to the glistening pay phone and just stared at it.

Some of this day was recounted to me by my older siblings, but there was one thing I knew at the time, one thing I will know and remember forever.

We were, at that moment, homeless. My mother had taken a bold, noble chance to keep us safe, and in doing so, pushed our lives to the limit, stretched us painfully toward survival . . . but then stopped short of going all the way. She couldn't finish the job. We had traveled nearly eight hundred miles and yet really had gotten nowhere. We were homeless.

As a family, we never embraced. Shows of open affection were considered signs of weakness. To fall into someone's arms meant that yours were not strong enough to hold yourself up. In our family, love was found not in shared sentiment, but in mutual survival.

Still, right about then, I remember really needing a hug. We all did. As darkness fell, and the cool desert winds began to whip around us, my mother shook her head, walked back inside, and picked up the phone. My older sister followed to listen. It may have been the hardest call of my mother's life. But it was also the strongest. My sister was listening.

"Hello, Pastor, we're in Las Cruces."

Pause.

"No, seriously we . . . are . . . in . . . Las Cruces."

Pause.

"Yes, Pastor, we need your help."

Within a half hour, a station wagon pulled up with the smiling pastor and jugs of water and a bunch of laughing kids and, out of the chill of fear, the warmth of life. We were no longer alone. We were no longer unwanted. We descended upon the pastor and his wife for, yes, hugs.

Years later, before every big wrestling match, I remembered the coolness of that water and the lightness of those smiles. I remembered how only in the final act of that phone call did my mother complete our daring journey. I remembered that without that selfless final push, nothing that came before that push mattered.

During the 2008 Olympics, I was known for the greatness

of my finishes. I was known for overcoming late deficits to pull unlikely victories from the palms of defeat. I was known as the ultimate closer. I was asked by everyone, Where did you learn this?

I told them I didn't learn it, I lived it. What I didn't tell them was that only those sitting with me and my homeless family on that gas station bench in Las Cruces would understand.

From no home to five different homes in two years. That was our Las Cruces experience. With every home, a new lesson. With every home, a new kind of humiliation.

Las Cruces is where I first learned about the necessary mobility that comes with poverty. House to house, leaving before the rent is due, sneaking out before the landlord shows up, rushing to the post office for the welfare check as soon as it comes in, starting fresh in another hovel down the street when the rent's due on the previous one. Las Cruces is where I first came to understand the anger that comes hand in hand with poverty, bellies aching after five days of only oatmeal and beans, tempers flaring at the hopelessness of that month's final food stamp.

Las Cruces is where I first understood poverty's pain, and where I eventually found an exit from that pain. I was only five years old, but I quickly realized and figured out that I would have to fight my way out. Some way, somehow.

The first round was the pastor's house.

There were a dozen kids and three adults in a tiny little house meant for a family of four. We fought over towels, fought over toilet paper, slept in the kitchen, slept in hallways. We were only there about a month until we got on our feet and could find our own place, but it felt like a year. Lovely family, but I was always stepping on someone or hitting them by accident, or not by accident. Little did we know that compared to the next year of our life, we were living in paradise.

The second round was the crack house.

It started when my mother was hired as a dishwasher at a Chinese restaurant. Because we were still all really too young to be left alone to look after ourselves, she needed to move us close to the restaurant so she could keep an eye on us while she worked. Turns out, there was a studio apartment in the parking lot next to the restaurant, next to an AutoZone. The Chinese folks who owned both the restaurant and the studio apartment let us live in the studio for cheap. We had no idea it would end up costing so much in other ways.

It had become a crack house. Seriously. It was tiny and dark with bars on the only window and used needles on the floor. We walked inside with all of our stuff and smelled the urine and felt the stench and my older brother Alonzo shouted something that none of us really understood until then.

"Damn, we really *are* poor," he shouted.

There was no heat in the ice-cold New Mexico winter, no air-conditioning in the nasty, hot New Mexico summer, no inside toilet, and funky electricity that blinked off and on like an uncontrolled Times Square. We had no furniture, of course—I told you we never really had furniture until I was a teenager, right?—so we swiped crates from a supermarket for chairs, and bundled up our beloved, trusty blankets for beds.

I was growing older now, and my new home became a place where I learned about the "finer" things in life.

In the crack house, I learned the importance of a good night's sleep. This lesson was learned because I had to literally fight to get one. Night would come, and we would all lie on the floor, seven people lined up side by side like dead people in a grave, seven people who would slowly start pushing and shoving to get the biggest chunk of blanket under our backs. And then after dividing up the blanket space, we would fight for the pillows. It was, up to that point, the most important fight of my life. There were four boys and two pillows and whoever hit harder in the beginning would sleep more soundly later. When I moved to the Olympic Training Center in Colorado Springs about ten years later, folks couldn't believe it was the first time I had ever owned my own pillow. I showed them some of the scars on my head from my siblings' nighttime tussles and said, "Believe."

In the crack house, I learned the importance of ignoring the elements, of mentally overcoming them. This lesson was learned because, during the summers, it would feel like one hundred degrees inside the sweatbox, and the only respite was sleeping on the roof. That's right, sometimes my brothers, sisters, and I would climb up on the tile roof of the tiny studio and sleep slanted but outside in the cooler night air. Often I would spend the entire night worrying that I would fall to my death, starting awake if I started to slide. My sister Gloria took it a step further, literally. She once stood up, walked in her sleep, and actually fell to the concrete below.

"What's going on out there?" shouted our mother.

"Gloria fell off the roof!" shouted Alonzo.

"I'm a little dirty, but fine!" shouted Gloria.

Not exactly routine bedtime conversation.

I also learned the importance of controlling your bowel movements. Because we just had one toilet for seven people, it was constantly in use, long lines, squirming struggles, that sort of thing. So we had a rule. Pee outside, shit inside. If it was cold outside in the middle of the night, you learned to hold it in. If there was brown water flowing from underneath the bathroom door, you learned to hold your shit.

It was in the crack house that I also learned about sex. Not through the birds and the bees or through an awkward talk with my mother, but through Uncle Chu-cho and Cousin Rey. They were eighteen-year-old relatives who had snuck across the border from Mexico and were occasionally living with us. They were wild-eyed guys, wackos who could barely take care of themselves, but when my mother took an extra job at a nut factory at night, they had to take care of us, and you know what that meant.

Let's connect the dots. Crack house, crazy young uncles . . . gangs? Yep, that's who started showing up every night for long and loud parties—Mexican gang members who loved to have sex with their women and mess with their mascot. That was me. Before I won an Olympic gold medal, I was a Mexican gang mascot.

It started one night when I heard some guy killing a woman in our bathroom. At least, that's what I thought he was doing. She was wailing, and he was thumping, and I ran and threw open the door and climbed on his back, trying to pull him off. I tried to save her.

"Get off me, you crazy little man!" shouted the guy.

"Stop hurting that girl!" I shouted back, pounding my little fists on his shoulders.

"I'm not hurting her; I'm loving her!" he shouted.

Oh.

So at age seven, I knew about coitus. And within days, I learned about coitus interruptus.

"Hey, little Henry, get out here," shouted one dude.

It was probably about three a.m., although that is totally a guess, because besides not having a television in the crack house, we also didn't have a clock.

"Little Henry, you gotta get up, get out here!" he shouted again.

I remember stumbling to the door in my underwear, into the tattooed arms of some greasy guy who smelled. He was pointing to the corner of the parking lot, where an old, abandoned convertible was bouncing around as if driving on a bumpy road. Except the car was in park.

"Little Henry, two people are in there screwing. Do you know about screwing?" he said.

Hell, thanks to my relatives, I was an expert at identifying it by this point.

"Little Henry, it's nighttime. Do you have to take a piss?" he said.

"Yeah," I said, still groggy.

"Good," he said. "Go over and climb on the hood of that car and take a piss."

"Where?" I said.

"On the two people who are screwing!" he said.

And so I did, hauling my little body on the chrome hood and sending a stream down upon the backseat that sheltered the couple. How romantic. I've done a lot of great wrestling moves since then, but nothing compared to the dexterity I showed while racing barefoot back to the crack house while pulling up my underwear.

I got cocky. Soon this little Mexican gang mascot was sticking a hose into cars, turning the water on, and flushing out screwing couples, throwing mud on screwing couples, jumping in front of windows and scaring screwing couples.

Lost in all this screwing was the fact that my childhood was being screwed up. I slept late, played little, hung out with gangsters, and fought every day to ignore the weed being smoked and cocaine being snorted. Sometimes I would make my escape with my mom—I was still too young for school—but even then, I would be leaving one fight for another fight.

The third round occurred in the chili fields.

Among my mother's other jobs in Las Cruces, she picked chilies. On the most wonderful, weird days, she would take me with her. We would pile into some stranger's truck and bump our way out to the chili fields, where my mother would spend the day with a basket around her shoulders, hunched over in the heat, grabbing the little red beasts off the bushes with her callused hands. I would follow her, grabbing and adding to the basket, helping her out as much as I could, happily close to the woman who was a role model for me not only in life, but in physical endurance and sports.

She was a role model in endurance, because she put up with things like the Great Chili Fight. One day she brought all the kids to help her, only Angel and I couldn't just quietly work; we started competing over who could pick the most chilies. Soon we were throwing chilies at each other and chasing each other around the bushes and causing a huge commotion, but even then, it would have been just a nice distraction. Until the chilies broke. And then we had chili stuff on our fingers, which meant it was soon in our eyes, which meant we were soon crying uncontrollably and rolling around the ground, begging God for mercy.

"Get out, all of you!" shouted the foreman.

My mother left that day without making any money. And she never returned with any of us again. But she never screamed at us for this, never punished us for this, never did anything but sigh and wish that life were different and that her children could have somewhere to play other than a chili field. My poor, sweet mother.

She was also my role model in sports, because she could run. Man, could she run. These fields are where I learned she could really sprint. One minute she would be hunched over, and the next minute somebody would shout, "*La Migra!*" and soon we would be sprinting down the long rows of bushes, jumping into someone's van, speeding away.

My mother was a legal worker here under the Amnesty Act. But she never trusted it, never trusted the people who could so casually send her back to Mexico, so whenever her friends ran, she ran too.

It was in Las Cruces that I realized that, while I was an American, I wasn't always so welcome in America. It was in Las Cruces that I saw the worst this country had to offer its poor, living in a crack house, running from the immigration police, supervised by two nuts, living mostly unattended and unwanted.

I remember the time my brother Alonzo and my uncle and cousin just disappeared. I came home late one night with my mother from one of her jobs and we counted three fewer dead-like bodies on the floor. I was happy to have a better chance at a pillow, and a few more feet of cover. I didn't realize then what had happened. But my mother sat up all night against the wall, worried, her eyes blinking in the dim streetlight that came through the barred window.

Turns out, my uncle and cousin were grabbed by immigration, and Alonzo had gone along with them because he didn't want them to be alone. They were driven about an hour down the road to the Mexican border, dumped off in the countryside, and immediately crossed back over the Rio Grande River on inner tubes, slept under a bridge in El Paso, and hitchhiked home the next day.

That was my first understanding of immigration laws. One day my family was being thrown out of the country, the next day they were back in the crack house cooking beans. Once immigration knew my two uncles were illegal, the guys in green jumpsuits were around the house all the time. I would awaken to sounds of my uncles shouting and footsteps churning up the gravel. I would look outside to see them being chased into the fields. I would awaken the next day to sounds of my uncles laughing and joking as they walked back into the house, their one-day forced visit to the homeland having ended.

To me, immigration laws are stupid. Immigration laws don't work. Think about it. If my parents had not been able to figure out how to come over to this country, I would never have been able to represent the United States in the Olympics. I would never have had that chance to help make this country shine brighter. It doesn't make sense.

My mother could not watch me in Beijing because she didn't have an American passport, because she wasn't officially an American citizen, just a permanent resident. Her official passport would have to come from Mexico, but darned if she was going back for it. So she stayed in the United States and stewed over the awful irony. She had worked sixty hours a week for two decades to support this country and her family, yet she wasn't worthy enough to watch her son wrestle for it?

My mother had a sister in Phoenix who kept calling us and offering help. My mother finally agreed to join her. When I climbed on another rickety bus for another move to anywhere and nowhere, I was carrying more than just a torn-up box full of our life's few possessions, more than just one of those colorful blankets. I was carrying a chip on my shoulder, a huge chip toward a country that I felt didn't want me, a family that couldn't take care of me, and a stomach that wouldn't stop growling.

On the way to Phoenix, in part rage and part boredom, my brothers and I fought. Only this time, it wasn't the playful pushing for a towel; it was the serious punching for a point. The bus bumped, and we wrestled, over and over.

The fight that had nastily grown with me, a fight that would scar my insides far deeper than anything on my face or head, had begun.

Not until fifteen years later, when I walked off that mat after my final Olympic match in Beijing, would the fighting end.

⋆FOUR⋆

The blue mat felt like our living room floor at home, only softer. The dank reek of sweat made it smell like our bedroom, only cleaner.

There I stood, on a cracked blue mat in a tiny gym, having raced down from the bleachers after watching my twelve-year-old big brother Angel use a wrestling match as an excuse to twist some poor kid into a pretzel.

There I was, at age ten, standing for the first time on what felt like my field of dreams.

What a place! What a miracle! Here, you could throw someone and not break a lamp. Here, you could pile-drive someone and not bust a door. Here, you could fight and not get yelled at. Here, you could actually fight and get cheered for it. Are you kidding me?

Other kids had also run down to the mat. Some were throwing around the huge wads of used wrestling tape left over from the match. Others were playing soccer with the smashed, empty Gatorade cups, kicking them around on the floor. I had the mat all to myself. Like I said, are you kidding me?

"Somebody wrestle me!" I screamed, my tiny voice causing giggles as I stood there in my jeans and T-shirt.

All around me, the remnants of my brother's junior wresting meet were dispersing. Exhausted parents were hustling their bruised little kids to the car. A guy with a broom was sweeping up the discarded Gatorade bottles in the corner.

But I was going nowhere. I was finally on my field of dreams, and I was ready to play.

"C'mon, who wants to wrestle!" I screamed again.

Finally, a bigger kid jumped out of the stands and jogged to the middle of the mat to face me. He then leaned over, poked me in the chest, shoved me in the shoulder, and put up his hands in a fighting stance. Funny, but he looked like Angel in the family room when we were fighting over the remote control. Or maybe he looked like Alonzo, in the bedroom when we were brawling over a pillow to sleep on. The only difference was that, suddenly, I could attack without recourse and hurt without remorse.

Are you kidding me?

Boom! I charged the kid and threw him to his stomach. Boom! I put him in a headlock and turned him on his back. Boom! I buried my shoulders into his shoulders and . . .

"Boys, boys!" shouted one of the parents. "Stop it! Now! The gym is closing and it's time to leave."

I stopped. But I never really stopped after that. After several years of home schooling in fighting, I had gotten my first taste of real wrestling, and it felt as tangy and intoxicating as the blood that leaked from the lip I had somehow bitten in my tussle.

"Just like at the house, huh, Henry?" said Angel, putting his arm around me as we walked out the door.

"Only better," I said.

Ten years old, and the story of Henry Cejudo, the wrestler, had officially begun.

The city was Phoenix, where we had moved three years earlier from Las Cruces. We had come, as always, looking, searching for a better life. Yet we had found and experienced, as always, only a marginal life and an exhausting, never-ending struggle.

My aunt had invited us, so we lived with her for a few weeks, then moved to a cousin's house, then moved to one cheap apartment, then to another cheap apartment, no jobs, little welfare, poor as always. Only now all the kids were in school, so we felt even poorer, seeing ourselves compared to our classmates every day.

Poor-As-Hell Moment, Scene One: I walked into a third-grade class without my math homework for the third straight day. When my teacher noticed that I was not passing up a paper with neat little lines of numbers on it with the rest of the kids, again, she stared at me and shook her head.

"Mr. Cejudo, this is three straight days without your homework. Is there a reason you are not doing it?"

"Yes, ma'am."

"And that is . . ."

"I can't see it."

"You can't see it?"

"We haven't have had electricity for two weeks."

Poor-As-Hell Moment, Scene Two: I walked into a classroom on the first day of fourth grade wearing the same raggedy clothes that were on my back on the final day of third grade. Only, since then, I had grown, and the clothes had shrunk, jeans hanging off my butt and a shirt curled around my little biceps. All around me were shiny new jeans and spotless new back-to-school tennis shoes. All around me were stares—I felt people looking at me like some kind of spectacle. One stare was from my teacher.

"Mr. Cejudo, can you tell us what you did this summer?"

"What do you mean?"

"Can you tell us where you went on your summer vacation?"

"Summer vacation?"

"You know, did your family take you to the beach in California, or to the Grand Canyon, or to the Washington Monument?"

"Oh, um, all of them."

"What do you mean?'

"We went to all those places."

She knew I was lying. Everyone knew I was lying. But at that point, the truth that I had spent the summer moving with my family to three different apartments while being pursued by two drunken landlords was too much to bear. And too embarrassing. School, in general, was too much to bear.

Try going to class, walking the halls, and sitting in the cafeteria when you are constantly the new kid in that class, changing schools every couple of months, everyone staring at your tiny size, misfit clothes, and soon shaking their heads at your quick temper. Thirteen schools. Think about that. Twelve grades, thirteen schools. Hell, I wasn't a student, I was a novelty, a trinket, a mascot, a little Spanglish-speaking kid respected by nobody. Is it any wonder, then, that I would fight anybody and everybody?

Officially, I guess, I would only fight anyone who was bigger than me or acted bigger than me. Unofficially, that meant pretty much everybody because I was so tiny. A kid laughed at me for tripping on a soccer field and falling down. Boom! A kid laughed at me for not being able to read aloud from our fifth-grade history book? Boom! When I wasn't changing schools, I was being suspended from schools. By the time I was eleven, I had already been held back two grades, so I was spending my days with strange little kids in strange giant classrooms and, well, is it any wonder that when I finally picked a sport, it was one of the most individual of sports? Wrestling is what you do when you don't want to be bothered with teammates. When you want to control your own situation and depend only on yourself and your own strength, your own limits. Avoiding the idea of teammates is something you do when you don't have any friends.

Not that I didn't like my schools. In fact, I loved them. Because I loved to eat, and school was where that happened more than anywhere else in my life until that point. I would get there early for the free breakfast, and stick around for every possible lunch period to eat what might be my last meal of the day. I swear, if schools served free dinner, I would never have gone home.

But, of course, all the schools wanted me out of there as soon as possible. On the way to school, every bus driver would make me sit up in the front next to him, where he could watch over me and scare me away from throwing spitballs and toilet paper and causing chaos. Before I left a school, each school counselor would talk to me about ADD, saying that I needed help, once even summoning my mother.

"Mrs. Cejudo," said the white psychologist in Spanish, so proud that she could relate to the poor forlorn parents of her students. "Your son needs ADD medicine."

My mom looked over at me in the adjoining chair, perched anxiously in this adult meeting; she balled up her fist, and gently placed it on the side of my head.

"*This* is his ADD medicine," she said, shaking that fist. When I returned home, she gave me the first of what I called my Adderall Ass Kickings. Her hand on the back of my head gave me my focus. Her stick across my butt quelled my hyperactivity.

I suffered from a lack of attention, all right. But it wasn't only my lack of attention, it was the lack of attention other people paid to me. Which is to say, none. I acted nuts and out of control because I needed that attention. I craved it. I needed that attention because I was always the new kid, flying under the radar, without a history. I would do anything to make people think I was somebody. I once even started the largest food fight in the history of our junior high, started it with one flick of a French fry. I was so proud.

I wanted people to see me as a shining light because, when I returned home each night, I was surrounded by darkness, and I'm not just talking about the lack of electricity.

It was in Phoenix where we once hustled out of our apartment with the rent due, climbed on a city bus, and rode it to nowhere.

"Get your things; we're going!" my mother shouted one afternoon in the all-too-familiar tone that was part strength and part panic. We knew to pay attention to her when she used that tone.

We had no furniture, remember, so our move was quick. We packed up the boxes with our clothes and other possessions and grabbed those damn blankets, and within an hour we were downstairs, standing outside on the apartment building's dying front lawn.

"We're getting on the bus," my mother announced, and away we marched, six sad ducklings staggering behind a lost, conflicted mother duck. We didn't ask where we were going. We never asked. We didn't want to know. Our stay there would only be bad and brief, so why bother?

This time, though, even my mother didn't know. She had no plan. I'll never forget how she jerked her head around on the bus, staring outside the window at vacancy signs and barred-window buildings, from side to side, as if trying to decide where to land.

While riding this bus up one of Phoenix's main drags, my mother seemingly ready to leave and jump off the bus at every stop, her head twitching as she looked back and forth, and her hands sweating, it finally hit us.

"You know something?" whispered my sister Gloria. "I think right now, at this moment, we are homeless."

Yes, for the second time in our life, we were truly homeless. Our mother finally pulled us off the bus at a stop next to a complex where we had once stayed with some friends. Believe it or not, as we dragged our stuff by the empty, dirt-streaked pool in the courtyard—maybe we were going to sleep in there?—we saw some of our old neighbors. They recognized us. They empathized with us. Turns out, they were also being evicted from their apartment. My mother pulled out her welfare check, they pulled out theirs, and they decided to pool their meager resources and share the one-bedroom tenement apartment so both families could survive and have a roof over their head for the time being.

Eight kids, four adults, one bedroom, one bathroom? Sometimes I think God made me so small because, throughout my young life, there was just never enough room. We just had to cram in.

It was also in Phoenix, incidentally, where we lived in a junkyard. People think I am joking about this when I mention it. But I'm as serious as a rusty fender.

We were in the process of moving on the promise that my mother's boyfriend had said he had a nice place we could share. Only, he was a liar, and his place turned out to be a mobile home in the back of a junkyard, barely big enough for one person, much less a whole troop like us. We had no choice, though, but to stay there a week until my mother's welfare check arrived, everyone sleeping in a row like canned sardines on the floor like always, the usual nightmarish nights, with one scary twist.

The bathroom was outside the mobile home. And there were two big, ferocious guard dogs roaming the junkyard outside that bathroom. That meant you better either be able to step fast or step soft if you wanted to relieve yourself. For all those wrestling opponents who will wonder how I am able to do both, well, this is where I learned. You try holding your piss while a slobbering, growling Cujo is on your butt. How could a slobbering, growling Russian be any worse?

The thicker the squalor, the bigger my dreams. It was in that junkyard trailer in the summer of 1996 where I first had the dream that would change my life and forever alter its course. It was August, and sweltering in the tiny tin can of a home, but the dogs were outside, so I had no choice but to spend this particular night sitting on one of our two milk crates—"I'll fight you for it!" I would shout to anyone in my family who called dibs on the crate—and watch TV. It just so happened that the TV was turned to the Atlanta Summer Olympics. My first Olympics. The most amazing Olympics.

I saw how ordinary people doing what I had previously considered ordinary things—things like running, jumping, fighting—could be showered with extraordinary love and turn these ordinary activities into extraordinary action and the highest honor. I saw them hugged where I was never hugged. I saw them cheered with the sort of roars I only heard from the backs of rickety busses. More than anything, I saw them loudly and publicly embraced by a country where I had never felt welcomed.

If you must have a name that stood out for me as an inspiration from that telecast, I'll give you a name. Michael Johnson. The way he flew around the track as if an entire country was pushing him, the way he later waved the American flag as if an entire country was holding him, I was hooked. Damn it, that was going to be me one day. I was going to hold that flag just like that. I was going to feel that love just like he did. I didn't know how, I didn't know when, I didn't even know how or what sport would get me there. But that day, as I sat in the stink of that sweatbox, I fell in love with the cleanliness, goodwill, and charm of the American Olympic dream.

At one point during the night, one of my brothers reached up to grab the set of pliers stuck into the TV that held it together and controlled the channels. He was going to turn the channel. I stopped him, rose from my milk carton seat, and pointed to the screen, which contained the wondrous sight of a filled stadium alive with the chanting sounds of "U-S-A! U-S-A!"

"I'm going there!" I announced to my family.

"Where? Atlanta?" asked my brother, slumped on the floor on a blanket.

"No, the Olympics!" I announced. "I'm going to win a gold medal."

I heard muffled chuckling and snickering from the corners of the trailer, and so, with a great sigh of disillusionment, I slowly sat down and took my place back on the crate.

"Shit!" What was that noise? "Owwww!" Who was there? Just as I finished my great Olympic prediction speech, there was a loud and painful cry from outside the trailer. The door suddenly swung open, a quick and frightened gasp was heard, then a disheveled teenage girl stumbled inside. It was one of my sisters, pulling up her pants as she slammed the door on hungry barking and angry growling. She had used the toilet and beaten the dogs by a nose. Literally.

"Now *that* is an Olympian," said one of my brothers.

I knew I was going to the Olympics in some sport when I watched it on TV back as a kid. I would always remember that moment and my brothers and sisters would too. I just didn't know I was going to wrestle at the Olympics, that that would be the path to realize my dreams, until I watched my brother Angel wrestle.

He was barely two years older than I was but, because my mother commanded us to take care of each other, he was as much father as brother. Everywhere I would go, he would take me with him: to the corner mini-mart for groceries, to sleepovers with friends—we were attached at the hip by decree from the boss.

And, man, how we would fight to separate. Siamese twins have undergone less pain in separating. In unleashing the aggression that was born in Las Cruces, our Phoenix days were bursting with brawls. We would attack each other with couch cushions, beating at each other's heads. We would wrestle each other on the kitchen floor. Angel and his friends would put me on a blanket and toss me in the air to see if I could land on my feet. If I did, I would use those feet to leap into his face and come at him with my fists. We broke dishes. We broke doors. We put holes in walls.

Once we fought so badly over an old Nintendo set, my mother pulled out a knife and cut the Nintendo cord to put an end to our incessant arguing. Another time we fought when we were supposed to be washing dishes, so my mother threw away all but one plate, one cup, one glass, and one set of silverware, to make a point. This way, anytime anybody wanted to eat, they had to wash a dish. I was surprised my mother could make such a symbolic stand when we were so stupendously poor, but she pulled it off.

"Angel, you are Cain and your brother is Abel!" she always shouted.

"C'mon, Mom, why do I have to always be the one who is killed?" I shouted back.

Angel once beat me up and then stole all my clothes, which really didn't bother me too much, because it was hot, and, after all, they used to be his clothes anyway. In return, I would beat up Angel in a staged fight like the World Wrestling Federation stuff we saw on TV; then I would refuse to let him beat me up, stalking away as if I really was tougher.

It was the WWF that got Angel interested in real wrestling, and raging hormones that made him give it a try. Just before Angel started sixth grade, his height and weight ballooned. He suddenly stood about five feet tall, nearly a half-foot taller than me. He suddenly weighed almost ninety pounds, which was several pounds more than me.

We couldn't fight each other fairly anymore. And it wasn't any fun to pretend otherwise. So Angel went to Pueblo Junior High and signed up for wrestling so he could fight against other kids his size. And he was good. He was the same guy in the living room beating up his little brother, only quicker and legal, and playing by some set rules for once.

I saw him winning tournaments and getting hugs from my mom, who, you know by now, rarely hugged. It was special to get a hug from her. I saw him being cheered by people who normally wouldn't talk to the poor Mexican kid on the streets. I saw the makings of another Michael Johnson, and I wanted to do that too.

So, after testing myself in pickup wrestling matches after his official matches, I decided to challenge Angel for real. Well, actually, I didn't have much of a choice. One summer day a guy came by the apartment. My mom wasn't home; she was never home. This was the summer that Angel was thirteen. I was eleven.

So we heard a knock on the torn screen door, and right about then Angel had me in a headlock over by the refrigerator, so he released me, got up, and walked to the front of the apartment and opened the door. And here's this guy, he was some middle-aged man we had seen hanging out during the wrestling matches. I think his name was Sal. So many people came in and out of our lives at that time. I wasn't too good with names.

"Dude," Sal (I think) said to my brother, noticing his sweat and my sweat, realizing that we had just been fighting. "If you really want to be a good wrestler, you got to train over at the Maryvale Club. There's this guy there, Frank Saenz, he'll take care of you. You need to work year-round."

Angel thought about this offer for a second, stared at the old dude with wonder while he considered it, and then looked down at me with disgust.

"I can come," he said, "but I gotta bring my little brother."

Wrestling history will probably be twisted to say that Angel recognized my wrestling prowess early on and insisted that I join him at Maryvale because he knew I was headed for greatness. Yeah, right. While Angel has been my biggest supporter over the years—he was even my wrestling partner in Beijing—his request to bring me to a wrestling club had nothing to do with wrestling. Bottom line, it was summer, and he had been placed in charge of me by our mother. He knew he would get whipped if he left me alone, so he had no choice. In the beginning, my brother was not being a benefactor, he was being a babysitter.

"Ah, sure," said Sal. "Bring the kid."

And that was that. I had earned my first ticket to a wrestling room. We jumped into an old truck and rattled about three miles down the road to a tiny cinder-block room attached to a local high school. We walked inside and were immediately overcome with the sensation of having walked into hell.

Or was it heaven?

Rap music thumped from the ceiling. Sweat rose from the two giant wrestling mats. Two ropes swung wildly from the ceiling. Two kids in wrestling singlets were climbing the ropes. All around them, other kids were running and jumping and carrying each other around the room until they collapsed. I saw one kid run from the room, through a far door, just before I heard the unmistakable sound of vomiting.

This wasn't a wrestling practice; this was a Friday afternoon at my house. This wasn't a sport; this was life as I already knew it. As Angel strutted over and took his place among the dripping-wet athletes, I sort of wandered around the edges, watching, until I was spotted by a round man with a big smile.

"Ain't you Angel's brother?" shouted the community treasure that I would come to know as Frank Saenz.

"Yep," I said.

"Then get dressed!" he said, pointing me toward a giant box of old and tattered wrestling gear.

It was the greatest shopping spree of my life, picking out a thick cotton singlet that fit my tiny body. The uniform smelled horribly but, then, so did I. It was threadbare and riddled with holes.

That was the beginning of my wrestling career, in a windowless room wearing secondhand clothes, and making little kids cry. Because that's what happened my entire first week on the Maryvale Wrestling Club. I would practice against other tough kids my size, and turn them into sniveling babies. Coach Saenz said he noticed me in practice at first because I didn't treat it like practice. I treated it like survival, like life or death. I would slam my elbow into noses, throw my knee into crotches, beat on somebody (legally for the first time in my life and without the danger of my mom yelling at me) and enjoy every moment of it.

They said I looked angry before practice, and relieved after practice. Like a weight had been lifted from my shoulders temporarily. They said I looked like I was in another world when I wrestled, and I was—I was in a world where I could get up off the mat, a world where I could do the hurting, a world very unlike my own off the mat.

Of course, this new world had its own laws. Wrestling isn't just about the strongest; it's about the quickest and smartest and most agile. And, no, unlike the wrestling that I used to watch on television, it was not okay to break a chair over someone's head or leap from a top rope down onto someone's skull. This was not professional wrestling. This was not entertainment. This was a serious sport.

This was you and an opponent climbing over each other for three two-minute rounds on a foam mat. You scored points by moves that would give you a physical advantage or show physical control. The most points were scored when you moved a guy from his feet to his back. The most dominating win was when you pushed that guy's shoulders to the mat and held them there for a second or so, resulting in a pin. But most matches are not so dramatic. Most matches are a marathon of clutching and grabbing and fighting for position.

It's the greatest martial arts sport because it's the one that uses every muscle in your body for every minute of the competition. The average person in average shape couldn't last more than one minute of one round in wrestling. It's like running ten miles while moving every part of your body and, at the same time, enduring somebody of equal weight hanging on your back and choking you.

The sport has been in the Olympics since 1904, in two different forms, freestyle and Greco-Roman. Freestyle is wrestling with all parts of the body. Greco-Roman is wrestling from the waist up. While I have won national junior championships in both forms of wrestling, I became strictly a freestyle wrestler because it's more popular and because I love using everything I've got.

But, as I learned quickly, the best part of wrestling is that wrestling room. For an entire year, from fifth to sixth grade, it seemed like I lived only for and in that room. I would jog three miles from my apartment after school, put on that nasty singlet, and work out until nine p.m., or until I could find somebody to give me a ride home, whichever came first.

I practiced on Christmas Day because I hated Christmas, remembering how my father once stole it from us. I practiced on Thanksgiving Day because, as Mexican Americans who received stares and scorn around town, it was hard to hold a feast honoring Pilgrims when we felt like the Indians. And, of course, I would always, always, always practice on Father's Day. Man, did I hate Father's Day. I would have a really good workout that day with all my extra energy. In class that week, the teacher would ask us to draw a picture portrait of our fathers. I would draw my mother, then crumple it up and want to go home sick. Fourth of July? More work. The only thing that ever happened on the Fourth of July in my house was the ceremonial burning of someone's fingers from those freaking sparklers, which we would light and immediately press to each other's skin. Yeah, I know, lovely, huh? It's a wonder I didn't skip the Olympics and go right to WrestleMania.

The only holiday on which I did not wrestle was Halloween. I loved it. Greatest holiday ever, Halloween. I could do two things on Halloween that I would never get to do during the rest of the year. I could walk around the neighborhood after dark, and I could get free candy! Not that I didn't also dress up. I always dressed up. I was always the same character, year after year. I would put on lipstick and a black garbage bag and, with my naturally crooked teeth, I would make quite a sight.

"And what are you?" asked the adults who opened the door when we trick-or-treated.

"I'm a bum vampire!" I would answer.

I had my first official wrestling match in sixth grade, at age twelve, and it was one of the most profitable matches of my life. I beat some rich kid, and a couple of months later he gave me his wrestling shoes, my first shoes that weren't used Keds.

My first wrestling loss, as you can imagine, took place shortly thereafter. The kid wasn't tougher than me, but he was smarter than me and fought smarter than I did. I leaped for him without thinking, like I always did back then, only he didn't cower; he twisted away in a deft move and eventually pinned me. Man, did I cry. I cried all night. I was a bad loser. I was really upset. But I had learned a good lesson. The wrestling room was a great place to lose your anger, as long as you could keep your head. I needed to calm down. I needed to realize that the winner wasn't being judged by bloodstains on the mat, but shoulders on the mat. By points. In order to rise faster, I had to move slower and smarter.

My first real teacher was a guy named Richard Fimbres. While Frank Saenz ran the Maryvale program, Richard often ran the practices, both in grade school and high school, and that meant he often worked with me, slapping me around to hold my attention, challenging me to keep working harder than the other kids, trying to control my instant cockiness, but, man, that was hard. I ended up winning my first six tournaments as a sixth grader and nobody could come close to me. I became good, strong, and even more cocky than usual. No shit could touch me that I couldn't handle. Literally.

I remember once during a practice when I was sitting in the one stall in the grimy high school bathroom across the gym from the wrestling room. Another wrestler was waiting outside the stall with dangerously rumbling bowels.

"Hurry up, dude! I gotta go!" he shouted.

"Ah, just go right there!" I yelled back at him.

So he did. I'm serious. My fellow wrestler dropped his singlet and went in the cracked urinal. Later that day, we were both pulled off the mat by Coach Saenz, who was screaming at us for fouling up the bathroom and demanding to know who was responsible. I said nothing. My empty-boweled buddy said nothing.

"Fine!" he shouted. "So you'll both go clean up the shit!!

My buddy refused, so the coach immediately kicked him off the team. There was no way I was leaving this room or the team, so I headed back to the john and cleaned it up myself, causing great consternation among my family, one of whom called Saenz and accused him of forcing me to do demeaning tasks for no reason.

"Henry, did you shit in the urinal?" Frank asked me later.

"No," I said.

"Then why didn't you tell me when it happened? Why did you clean it up?" he said.

"I didn't want to lose a friend," I said. "And then I didn't want to lose a wrestling room."

Man, I loved that place.

I not only loved the room, I desperately needed that room. I fought for that room. I slept in that room. I grew up in that room, one huge drop of sweat at a time. I lived in that room.

If Coach Frank or Coach Richard wanted us to do two sets of twenty-five sit-ups, I would do fifty. If he wanted us to climb the rope three times, I would do it six. If he wanted us to wrestle four different opponents, I would wrestle eight.

I was desperate for the outlet. I was desperate for the attention and care. I was desperate for the love. For a family that lived in such close quarters for so much of my young life, you would think the Cejudos would be comfortable with affection and touch. We weren't. We slept on top of each other, but we never hugged or showed much affection. We would spend all night talking to each other, but we never said, "I love you." For being such a physical family, we were not a physically loving family.

Some people don't need that affirmation. I wasn't one of those people. I needed a pat on the back, an arm around the shoulder, somebody to tell me I was cool and smart and worth it. All those people running around all the cramped spaces of my life, and it was like nobody ever took time to slow down and notice me.

I needed the ooohs. I needed the aaahs. I needed the cheers that came with greatness, and the hugs that came with distress.

Feeling alone for so much of my growing up, I needed to be surrounded in love.

Which may explain the craps game.

I loved the wrestling room, but soon I needed more. I needed another outlet. Having grown tired of seeing me bloody the same old noses, Coach Frank added me to the Maryvale Wrestling Club's traveling team. He would take us all over the Southwest in search of meets where we would get good competition. Albuquerque, Denver, El Paso, San Diego. It wasn't luxury travel by any means. It wasn't even economy travel. In the plane of life, we sat in the poverty section. We would all pile into one rickety van and stay in one crummy motel room all together, and then beat the crap out of a bunch of strangers. Quick, cramped, and ugly, all those trips. Yet I loved them all because, for three days, that ugliness made me feel beautiful and powerful. For three days, as long as I was winning, everyone was looking at me and complimenting me and making me feel like I owned the club. As the owner, of course, I reserved the right to arrange the entertainment.

So during a truck stop outside of Denver once during one of our away trips, I held a craps game.

It wasn't a big deal; it was just a bunch of kids gathered around me in a corner of the parking lot back by the men's room in whatever light we could find. But none of them really understood craps, whereas I had played it for ages in that infamous apartment courtyard with the old men. And I also owned the dice. And by the time it took Frank to use the bathroom and go inside to buy some cheap soda and trail mix for snacks, I had won most of the kids' spending money. As I recall, it was nearly fifty dollars, which was more money than an eighth grader like me had ever seen in his life, or had for all his own. It was so much money, I held it out and fanned it out and raised it up and . . .

"What the hell are you doing!" Coach Frank shouted, running over to me from the van.

"What?" I asked.

"You won that money from those kids in craps?" he shouted, grabbing at the money.

"Fair and square!" I shouted back, pulling the wad of cash away from him.

"You got two choices," he said. "Give me the money or walk back to Arizona."

"I ain't scared of you!" I yelled at him.

"Give me the money!" he hollered back.

"I ain't scared of shit!" I shouted.

"The money!" he shouted back.

So, yeah, okay, I gave him the money in the end. I would run three miles to the wrestling room, but I wasn't dumb enough to think I could walk across two states or piss off Coach Frank. Still, I'll never forget how that money felt in my hand. I'll never forget the anger I felt in seeing it leave my hand and get returned to its original owners.

"One day, that will all be mine!" I yelled as I climbed back in the van, and if you think this hungry Mexican-American kid didn't blatantly know he was poor at that moment and feel it keenly, you're wrong.

I hated to lose. Money, matches, respect, anything. I only lost three times in high school, but I lost other times in national tournaments, and each one was a nightmare, first for me, then for everyone else around me who had to deal with the fallout.

I already wrote about crying after my first loss, right? Then there was the time I finished second to this national stud Nick Galick in a big local tournament. I was only a freshman in high school, and he was older, but it didn't matter to me. I still felt that I should have beaten him.

I was so mad, I slapped his hand instead of shaking it after the match. I slapped his coach's hand instead of shaking it. I took my headgear off and threw it off the mat, threw my second-place medal into the stands, and ran off with the crowd booing, Coach Frank following after me.

"What the hell is wrong with you!" he shouted.

"Don't you understand?" I said. "I have to win! For me, there is no second place. Second place is the streets! Second place is the shits! I have to win!"

At that same time, Coach Richard was outside screaming at the fans and gathering all the ammunition he needed for the pep talks he would give me during my first two years in high school.

"People want to see you fail," he would tell me before every big match. "People think you don't deserve it. People don't think you are worth it. Everybody wants you to get punked. Prove everybody wrong."

For some, that would have been just an idle pep talk. But to me, it was real. Nobody really thought a poor kid with borrowed shoes and a torn singlet deserved to be among the best wrestlers in the country. From the very beginning, this lack of faith was my fuel.

Not that it always worked. I also remember a time in Reno, in an invitational tournament, when I got beat by some fool who had no business beating me. The way I lost that match was the way I lost every match that I didn't out-and-out win. I swung for the fences and missed. I threw the Hail Mary pass and it fell incomplete. I went for the kill and was killed. Coaches have continually tried to change me and change this impulse in me, but I had to be me. I was overly aggressive. I was way too daring. But I was far too stubborn—and smart—to change. Everyone told me I was good enough to sit back and be careful, but didn't they know that I became that good by charging out and fighting tooth and nail until the end? I risked everything in every match because, well, shit, what did I have to lose? Only my ticket out of the barrio, I guess.

Anyway, once in a while this strategy backfired. So we're in Reno, and I get beat, and I was supposed to stick around for the wrestle-backs, in which I would wrestle a bunch of other fellow losers for the right to a bronze medal and a consolation prize. Bronze medal? Screw that. I picked up my stuff, walked out into the surprisingly chilly night air, and hiked back to the motel. It was about a four-mile trek, but I didn't realize that at the time when I set out, fuming. I remember being cold and tired and furious. Then, about two hours later, I was in big trouble. Coach Frank had driven back to the one room we all shared at the Motel 3—or whatever the hell it was—and when I arrived back at the room, he was up in my face.

"You little screwup!" he shouted. "What am I going to do with you!"

"Make it so I don't lose again!" I shouted back.

Once I started hanging with Tracy Greiff, a volunteer coach and friend who I met just before I started high school, he and I figured out a better way for me to deal with these losses.

During my first two years of high school, Tracy would write down the name of every guy who might have a chance to beat me. Then he would check every wrestling schedule every weekend. If that guy was going to be in a tournament in Tucson or somewhere nearby, we would track him down and I would offer to wrestle him after the tournament. Or if the guy was training with the Arizona State team in Tempe, for instance, we would drive over there and challenge him after practice.

Every time, I would wrestle the guy until I knew I could beat him. Often there weren't any referees or scoreboards around, so usually we never knew who officially won. But I would wrestle until I knew in my heart and for myself that I could win the next time we met. It was as much mental as physical.

Fast-forward to the 2008 Olympic Trials. I ended up winning the trials and going to the Olympics by beating a former Olympian named Steven Abas. Well, guess what? Abas once beat me, and I used the same street revenge mental tactics on him. I practiced with him over and over until I knew I could beat him, and then I did—when it mattered. I also had another advantage over Abas. Years earlier, when I was just a punk and he was a star and we crossed paths at a meet, Tracy asked me if I wanted to be introduced to him. I said no, because I knew I would have to fight him one day. At that moment, he became the hunted and I became the hunter. And I felt I had a mental advantage over him.

I loved being a hunter. I would wrestle anybody, anywhere. Coach Frank took this desire and drive seriously and would utilize it. We would go to tournaments and, after I won the tournament, we'd be sitting in the stands watching other winners from other weight classes hang out around the mat.

"Hey, look at that kid staring up here. He thinks he can beat you," Coach Frank would say to me, almost taunting me.

Hell, the kid was probably checking out some chick sitting behind me, but I believed my coach, and I found my anger, and I would walk down to challenge him. And quite often, he would accept and we would end up wrestling. Sometimes my best matches were wrestled with no referee around, nobody watching, and nowhere near the main mat. I would toss kids into water fountains, and they would throw me into nearby lingering cheerleaders watching our aftershow. We would be rolling around in a darkened area of the gym where folks could only hear our grunts.

Then there was the time in San Diego that a kid really did talk shit to me. Some small, redheaded, freckled guy who I had beaten earlier in the tournament thought he had been screwed by the referee, and wanted the chance to get another shot at me.

"Get down here, pussy!" he screamed at me.

At the time, my match long since finished, I was dressed in jeans, T-shirt, and tennis shoes. For most kids, this is lounge wear for wearing after school or on the weekends. But for me, well, everything is fightin' wear.

So I went down there and beat the freckles out of the kid, threw him on his back, and pinned him pretty quickly, then watched him scamper away. I remained on the mat, kneeling down, rubbing the sweat out of my eyes, when I looked up and saw the same kid in a different-colored singlet, looking all fresh and ready to fight me again.

"You want some more of this?" I asked him.

"Bring it on," he said in a voice that sounded, well, a bit different.

Anyway, we started wrestling all over again and I was stunned that this kid I had just beaten was suddenly strong and fresh. He was all over me like he hadn't wrestled in a week, threw me on my back, took away my breath, jumped on me, and pinned me in about two minutes. What the hell? How did this happen? Was this kid a hustler? Did he jake the first match so he could whip me in the second match?

Once again, I knelt on the mat trying to catch my breath when I look up and think I'm having a stroke, because I'm sure that I'm seeing double. The guy I beat in the first match was walking out of the tournament with the guy that beat me in the second match. Two identical red-haired, freckled kids.

"Twins!" shouted one of their friends, pointing at them and laughing hysterically until I chased them all out of the building.

I shouldn't have been surprised that Coach Frank was always trying to set me up with guys to wrestle and take out my aggression on. He knew that if I wasn't wrestling in the gyms, I would be wrestling at home and causing a ruckus. I remember one time when he brought me home from practice, my sister was having a birthday party, and the entire living room was cleared out, none of the furniture we had just rented was inside, just a rug on the ground and a bunch of kids standing around the edge of the rug and my mom standing in the middle.

"What is she doing?" asked Coach Frank.

"I think she is refereeing," I said.

Sure enough, my cousins were taking turns wrestling each other, and my mom was making the matches and calling the shots.

"Holy shit," said Coach Frank.

"Welcome to my world," I said.

It was at that this point that Coach Frank pulled me aside and put an abrupt end to one of my early traditions. Remember in an earlier chapter when I wrote about wrestling kids in the Phoenix apartment courtyard for fifty cents? Well, I was still fooling around with that stuff.

"Henry, you've got to stop that," he told me as I entered my freshman year of high school. "You are better than that."

Better than something? Who? Me? I had never been told I was better than anything. That's why I always felt like I had to show it. But now Coach Frank believed it and he was flat-out telling me so. And, judging from my mother's choice of birthday entertainment, she also finally believed it.

My mother had gone from tolerating my wrestling to supporting it to the best of her ability, even embracing it. She had taken to selling food around the clock to help pay for our thirty-dollar wrestling cards or our McDonald's dinners when we were on the road. She would sell tamales out of the house, sell them to everyone in the apartment complex. When business was slow, she would push a cart along the side of the street selling oranges and corn to whoever would stop.

I'll never forget the time Coach Frank was driving us home and we spied my mom with her cart on the street corner, a hunched-over woman with lines in her face and tangles in her hair, selling food like a bum. She was not a bum. She was our saint, our savior, my mom. But still, being a fifteen-year-old high school freshman, I was embarrassed.

"Hey, Henry, is that . . . ?" said Coach Frank, looking in her direction.

"No, no, no, she's home," I said.

Years later, I am still ashamed that I denied her like that. And I am ashamed of being ashamed. We were poor. We were sometimes homeless. We fought like animals. We ate like starving dogs. So what? We never cheated. We didn't steal. We always survived somehow.

Actually, in order to pay for our wrestling trips, I did the same thing as my mother. I sold food. Only, I didn't do it out of a shopping cart on the corner of Forty-third and Thomas. I did it out of a box at Bank One Ballpark. I sold lemonade and hot chocolate at Arizona Diamondbacks baseball games and monster truck rallies and anything else that happened there. There was a guy who worked there who knew Coach Frank, and he set us kids up with occasional jobs walking through the stadium lugging huge containers of the liquids, which led to some unusual sightings. I mean, the hot chocolate barrel was bigger than I was. But my voice was bigger than all of it. I sold more of the stuff than anyone, because I shouted louder than anyone, and I could go all game, walking up and down the stadium steps. It was great exercise and I was already in great shape. Carrying a load of watery lemonade is nothing compared to carrying a 120-pound wrestler.

When we weren't selling sweets and concessions, we were selling parking spots. Actually, my man Tracy was selling parking spots while I was helping him. Before big events at the ballpark, Tracy would scour downtown businesses that had empty lots and knock on their doors, asking if they would donate their vacant lot to a bunch of poor Mexican kids who wanted to wrestle. He would then hold up signs outside of the lots charging twenty dollars to park. If the lot next to ours charged ten dollars,

I would hold our sign positioned in front of their sign so drivers looking for a spot wouldn't see the cheaper option.

We did anything to travel to meets. And then once we traveled, well, like I said earlier, we did anything. I remember once the police had to be called to our tiny San Diego motel room to break up a pillow fight. Maybe that's because one of the pillows was filled with shoes, and one of the wrestlers was beating the crap out of everyone with it.

Another time, when I was in Omaha, Nebraska, with Tracy and two other wrestlers, the police were summoned again. They pulled me over while I was driving a rented Ford Taurus into a giant shopping mall. I was stopped for speeding, but there were other complications.

Like, the only person authorized to drive the car was Tracy. And he was back in the motel room sleeping. And, oh yeah, we had sneaked out to meet some girls. Plus, I had no idea how to drive.

"We should take you kids to jail," said the policeman.

"Please do," I pleaded with him.

"Don't get smart with me," said the policeman.

"I'm serious," I said. "I'd rather sit behind bars than stand in front of Tracy."

I guess this is a good time to explain Tracy Greiff. He is a former wrestler who moved from Wisconsin to Arizona to start an insurance business. He is twenty years older than me, but he could still move and loved wrestling, so he showed up one day at one of our summer clinics between my seventh and eighth grade years, volunteering to help coach wrestling.

My brother Angel wrestled him first, and kicked his butt;

then they introduced Tracy to me, and told him that I was going to be even better. Tracy must have been impressed, because he started working with me, pushing me, making me consider ideas and strategies that I've never thought about before, like those lists where I would stalk everyone who had beaten me until I wasn't afraid of them anymore.

Before too long, Tracy was placed in charge of driving me and Angel to the clinics, then dropping us off at home, although we never actually let him drop us off at our real house, because we didn't live in the right district for Maryvale High. He dropped us off several blocks away and we would walk home.

Tracy wasn't the first guy from the outside who hung around me. I knew about people who realized that I might be good one day, really good, and wanted to help me. I was wary of these people for good reason.

But Tracy wasn't like that. He never asked for anything. He never wanted to barge in on my family—heck, for a long time, he never even dropped us off at our real house. After Coach Frank, he was the first person in my life to help me unconditionally, wrestler-to-wrestler, and helping me was never easy.

Just driving us to practices and clinics was a pain, because he didn't know where we lived and didn't pick us up at home, and half the time our cell phones were either broken or shut off for lack of payment. Sometimes he would have to drive around strange neighborhoods looking for a little kid walking along in wrestling clothes. If we found each other it would be by accident. Other times he would have to stop at every Circle K for a mile looking for a little kid using his last pennies on a candy bar, a kid who had forgotten about the time and would have missed the practice if Tracy hadn't been on him and taken him there.

After about six months, when we finally trusted Tracy, we let him take us to our real house and see what it was like. It was then that he said he first realized that either Angel or I would have to be a champion wrestler. He said there was no other explanation for how the house looked.

"Oh man," he said as he walked through our front door for the first time.

At his feet was ripped-up carpeting. Directly in front of him was a kitchen island with a missing countertop. Down the hall, huge chunks of the floor were gone. And the doors, well, they were an unhinged disaster. Some of them were busted and lying on the floor. Others were adorned with huge holes.

"How did all this happen?" he asked me.

"How do you think?" I said.

"Wow, you guys really do live wrestling," he said.

Once he saw this, Tracy started helping us live better, giving me money for food, rides whenever I got stuck, finding me old wrestling clothes, paying my annual wrestling fee.

When I was in eighth grade, it was Tracy who took me to my first movie. It was Tracy who took me to my first decent restaurant, scolding me when I ate four pieces of pizza before anyone else finished one, not understanding that eternally hungry people aren't used to eating slowly.

It was Tracy who started driving me to the really big meets that were sometimes miles away, like the nationals in Fargo,

North Dakota, taking me even though I had no ID, no phone, no money, nothing. He would take care of everything—I was a cause for him and he always had everything planned out.

Except, of course, the part of the plan about hiding his car keys when he slept.

So on that cold Omaha night, you can imagine my fear of the police bringing me back to Tracy and making me face the man from whom I had just "borrowed" a car and stepped out of line, the man to whom I owed everything. I'll never forget sitting in the back of the cop car while the cop banged on our Motel 4½ door and Tracy opened it in blue pajamas and bleary eyes. I could hear them talk through the open front window of the cop car.

"Do you know a Henry Cejudo?" the cop asked him.

"Yeah, he's in here sleeping," said Tracy.

"Are you sure?" said the cop.

At that point, I saw Tracy disappear for a second, then reappear at the door looking flustered and worried.

"Don't worry," said the cop, pointing out to the car. "We've got him right here."

At that point, the police released us and we raced past Tracy into the motel room. All of three of us climbed into one double bed, leaving Tracy alone to sleep in the other one. There was no way we were going near him and facing him after what we had pulled that night. As he returned from talking to the police, all three of us began loudly snoring as if sleeping. Looking at us briefly, sadly, shaking his head, Tracy then climbed into bed and turned his back and also started snoring.

He never said another word to us the entire trip. We awoke

the next morning, went to the tournament, won a bunch of matches with Tracy in our corner, but he didn't speak to us once. Not during the wrestling, not during the award ceremony when we accepted a bunch of medals, and not even once during the eighteen-hour drive home.

It was the worst thing. It was exactly how you kill me. You ignore me. You don't talk to me. You don't listen to me. You marginalize me and shut me out. It is exactly what Tracy did, and it worked. I have never felt more sorry for hurting someone ever, never felt more soundly punished.

A few days later, I heard a honk outside our house, and it was Tracy, driving me to practice, only he was talking to me again, acting like nothing ever happened. To this day, we have never spoken about the incident. But, to this day, I have never been scolded louder and have never felt worse about letting him down.

Yeah, at that time of my life, I was a bit of a jerk. Where Tracy would ignore me, Coach Frank would kick my butt, throwing me out of the cab of his truck and making me sit in the back in the freezing weather if I didn't shut up or play by the rules. Now that I think of it, I probably spent about half of my eighth grade year sitting in the back of that damn truck.

But I worked. Man, would I work. I would work three hours in the wrestling room, then go over to a health club nearby, sneak in, and work another hour. Once, during part of a six-and-a-half-mile run up South Mountain, I grabbed one of our coaches and carried him on my back. Coach Frank went crazy with excitement, and soon the entire team was carrying someone on their backs. On that same mountain run, I once got bored and hitchhiked to the top instead of running there. Of course, I got caught. And of course, I ended up in the back of the truck.

During this time, I started to rack up the titles. I know they don't mean much to people who don't wrestle—hell, I never heard of half these titles—but they got me noticed. And remember, I was all about being noticed.

In 2001, in eighth grade, I was the state junior high champion in Arizona.

In 2002, in ninth grade, I won five national titles in Greco-Roman, freestyle, and collegiate-style wrestling. I also went 35–2 for Maryvale High and won the state championship at 103 pounds.

In 2003, in tenth grade, I won more national titles while, back in Arizona, I was 38–1 and won the state title at 119 pounds.

About the only thing that didn't work out for me when it came to wrestling was my right ear. Have you seen my right ear? It looks like a little baseball mitt, all puffed out and covered in grooves. Even the casual wrestling fan will say it looks like something else. Of course, like a piece of cauliflower.

This is a cliché part of this book, but it's true—I have the curse of every wrestler. I have a cauliflower ear. It comes from the ear being constantly batted and pounded and slammed into a mat. It appeared in eighth grade, and puffed up so bad that I had to have it drained about thirty times by coaches in the bathrooms outside wrestling rooms. How would they do it? With a dog needle purchased from a pet store.

It's disgusting. It's unattractive. I know this. But I also know, it's me—it's part of me. It's almost like a badge for me. If you hang around me for more than ten minutes, and I catch you looking at the ear—everyone does—then I will ask you if you want to touch it. I will. And you should. It's the strangest thing. It's like touching a piece of wood. It's rock hard. You can rap it with your fist, and it's like rapping the top of a hard table.

The first question is always, "Can you hear out of that thing?" My answer is always, "Would I be answering you if I couldn't?" I can hear out of it perfectly.

And even though I was just a freshman, I could hear my days in Phoenix winding down and ending.

It started, as everything with me started back then, with Angel. While I was making a name for myself in police cars and baseball parks and still working my way up in the wrestling world, he was becoming probably the best high school wrestler in the history of Arizona. In four years, he won four state championships and was never beaten once—*not once!*

He was incredible. But he was also getting burned out. He got a girlfriend—I would never dream of a girlfriend then, because I dreamed only of ass whippings—and he got bored and lazy.

Even though he was unbeaten, he would never work out as hard as me, and I would scream at him for it.

"What's wrong? Don't you want to win?" I shouted.

"Just wait," he said, his eyes darting, his attention gone. "One day this will be you."

I prayed that would never be me. And then I just prayed for Angel, who messed around at school and couldn't score enough on the SAT test to attend any of the dozens of major colleges that were recruiting him and wanting him to wrestle for their teams.

So, suddenly, instead, the folks at United States Wrestling started recruiting him to be one of the pioneers in a new program they were starting.

For years, our country's wrestling program has lagged behind other countries' programs because our wrestlers usually spend four years in college, where the folkstyle wrestling is different from international freestyle wrestling in both technique and scoring. Our wrestlers participate in freestyle only in spring and summer in events sanctioned by USA Wrestling while wrestlers in other countries practice that style throughout the year. Why don't our high schools and colleges join the rest of the world? Good question. It's mostly because we've used folkstyle for many years, and the rules have become very traditional, and they work from middle school through college, while the worldwide freestyle rules are always changing. It works for us, but when our guys leave college at age twenty-two, it takes them several years to perfect the freestyle wrestling done by the rest of the world so they can compete effectively against them. So our Olympic champions—there have been forty-seven total since 1904—are usually all at least twenty-seven or twenty-eight years old.

Doc Bennett, the retired developmental freestyle coach of U.S. Wrestling, got the bright idea to bring kids to the Olympics Training Center before they went to college, teach them freestyle there, and get them on the mat at the Olympics at a younger, more competitive age. Anyway, that was the plan. And Angel was going to be part of that plan.

As they were recruiting him to go to Colorado Springs, I was getting fed up with Phoenix. After winning my second state championship after my sophomore season, I celebrated by running around flashing an "M" sign for Maryvale. Believe it or not, wrestling officials went crazy, accusing me of throwing gang signs.

If I had been rich and white, would that have happened? If I lived in a nicer area than the crumbling neighborhoods near Maryvale, probably nobody would have said anything. But once again, I felt I was being judged by my race and background, in an area of the country that should know better.

While being driven home from the tournament, I passed real Mexican gangs near my apartment, kids sitting on the curb with white tank-top undershirts and brightly colored boxers riding up their ass. They were always there. They looked menacingly at me. *Who is this tiny, punky high school kid who ignores us? What, he wrestles? So what? He should join us, wrestle for the streets.*

So great. I had just won a wrestling championship in a world that wrongly confused excited school spirit for a menacing gang sign, then returned to a world where real gangs wanted to steal my school spirit. Shit, I couldn't win. After just two years of high school, I was already moving close to a place from where I could never truly escape from the frustration and poverty I experienced daily.

I started thinking about getting out. I didn't know where, or how, but I knew I needed to get out, change my circumstances, make something happen.

Then it happened. Or, at least, I thought it happened. It felt like it was happening. In the early summer after my sophomore year of high school, I received a call from a USA Wrestling official asking me to practice with one of their national stars in Phoenix. What, me? Practice with an Olympian? At the same time my brother was being recruited by the Olympians? Hell, I've been attached to his hip my entire life. Maybe this latest request would allow him to carry me with him to his next glory. Could this practice session be my ticket out of Phoenix and on to something greater, something that looks like Michael Johnson?

"Wow, I'd love to wrestle your star," I said.

"You'll meet her next week, then," said the official.

Pause.

"Her?"

★FIVE★

Her name was Patricia Miranda. She had piercing eyes and a giant smile and a passion that I'd never seen before. Her hugs were incredible, her touch was electric, and within three minutes, she'd change my life.

Her name was Patricia Miranda, and she was the first woman who allowed me to kick her butt.

Now wait a minute here. I think I know what you are thinking. But you are so wrong. Patricia wasn't my girlfriend—she was my wrestling partner, an Olympian who became the first person to show the folks on the U.S. team that I could also be an Olympian.

It was the spring of my sophomore year in high school and I was a two-time state champion, one of the hottest tiny wrestlers in the country. Patricia was my size—about 105 pounds—but a giant in her sport of female wrestling. While wrestling for

Stanford, she was only the second female to ever beat a male in a Division I college match. She had since become one of the best female wrestlers in the world, and at that time was training for the 2004 Olympics in Athens, Greece.

Our paths crossed when her training brought her to one of my own training spots, a Phoenix high school where the wrestling room was run by former Olympic star Townsend Saunders. I worked with Saunders during the summer to stay in shape. She had flown down to work with Saunders that summer because he was going to be one of her national coaches.

She only had about four days to spend in town, so she wanted to work hard and fast and get the most out of the experience and her time with Saunders. Like any female wrestler, she knew exactly how to make that happen.

"She needs a man," Tracy observed to me one afternoon.

"She needs a, um, er, man?" I asked him back, confused.

I may have been a high school sophomore, but I was still tiny. I looked like a child. And I sort of still acted like a child too. As best I could tell, I had yet to even go through puberty, a fact which I mentioned to Tracy.

"That's exactly what she wants," he said.

"She wants to fight a little boy?" I asked.

"No, no, no," he said. "She wants to fight a tough high school kid who doesn't yet have his man strength."

This was a statement which, of course, raised an obvious question in my prepubescent mind.

"What the hell is man strength?"

Tracy then explained that because women's wrestling was still a relatively new sport—in fact, it would be making its Olympic debut in 2004—the serious female wrestlers had to search hard for suitable competition. There just weren't enough women competitors to go around and mix up the competition at a high level. So they looked for men. Actually, boys, high school boys who had not yet fully developed the muscles that the women would never have. So, yeah, boys like me.

"You are strong, but you still don't have your *man* strength," Tracy explained to me.

Whatever. I knew I had my man sweat, and my man stubbornness, and I knew that I would do whatever it took to avoid being beaten by this woman. Tracy drove me to the gym and I spotted her in the corner. She was my height, but she was about eight years older. However, she still looked pretty young and innocent, and actually she was quite cute, and suddenly I got sort of scared and nervous.

Not that I would lose the match, but that I would lose my emotional and physical grip.

In other words, what would happen if I touched her boobs?

It turns out, this weird fear is shared by many boys when it comes to wrestling women. That's one reason why it's been so hard for the sport to get a footing in this country. Because most women wrestle on boys' team on the high school level, there is quite a bit of coed romping, and quite a bit of parental angst about it. Some parents of boys don't feel their sons are ready for the trauma of, well, touching a girl's boob or body in the close way that you need to in order to wrestle them. Other parents feel their sons are placed in no-win situations when they wrestle with women—if the boy loses, he is humiliated, and if he wins, well, he was supposed to win, so no glory in that.

Once (I later learned) Patricia was coming off the mat after whipping some high school kid and his mother confronted her, screaming at her about how her son's life was now over. Patricia responded with, "You're doing a great job of raising your son to be an accepting, understanding, sensitive male. That's just great, teaching him that the worst thing that could happen to him in life is losing to a girl!"

That's what I liked about Patricia. She was smart. But even though I liked her and she was a woman, that still didn't mean I didn't want to kick her butt. And that still didn't answer the question—what if I touched her boob?

The answer, as all wrestlers learn, is that there are no real wrestling moves that would ever cause you to grab someone's chest. So no, I wasn't going to become the first guy to play two sports at the same time—wrestling and reaching first base. As I learned from Patricia, boobs are actually just a pain in the butt for women wrestlers, globs of fat that cannot help you outmuscle anybody.

"Except, of course, if the boobs are huge," Patricia once told me. "Then, I guess, you can smother your opponent."

Like I said, she was a great girl, funny and real. And she was a tough-as-nails wrestler. The only thing different about wrestling with her, and all women wrestlers, was that her singlet was cut higher under her arms, so opponents' hands wouldn't get caught in her sports bra.

But everything else was the same. She dove, she grabbed, she fought, and before I knew it, my fighter instincts were kicking in and I was naturally fighting back. We were supposed to begin with a normal wrestling practice, but soon it became takedown after takedown. There was little technique at that point. We were just going after each other. It was a hoot.

After about an hour, I looked up, and all the coaches were staring and shaking their heads and I thought, Wow, did she beat me up that bad?

"Unbelievable," said one coach.

"A high school sophomore?" said another coach.

Turns out, though, they were staring at me. Apparently, during that sweaty hour, she only scored, like, one point against me. Apparently all those takedowns were me taking *her* down, not the other way around. I was so distracted by wrestling a woman and having fun doing it that I didn't even realize I was beating her up.

I also didn't have a chance to look up in the stands and realize that the coaches were loving it. To be more exact, they were loving *me*. A new discovery.

One of them immediately summoned Tracy over for a quick conference.

"Get this kid over here every day for the next four days to keep working with Patricia," he told Tracy.

"Easier said than done," said Tracy.

You see, as I was getting older and more mobile, I was getting more difficult for Tracy to track down and corral. I was a high school kid with the schedule of an adult, but with the resources of a kindergartner.

First, my wallet. I didn't have one. I didn't need one. I had no ID card, and I had no money, so why would I need a wallet?

Second, my pockets. I didn't have any. I wore only gym shorts or sweats, usually cheap, often secondhand stuff, and none of them had pockets or pouches. I was lucky my shirts even had sleeves!

So for my first two years of high school, I walked around

town with everything tucked away for safekeeping in my socks. My house keys, my loose spare change, my wrestling card, everything. I know, brilliant, huh? It worked great if I was standing still and upright. But how much of my life is spent standing still? It would also have worked better if my socks had actually fit and weren't worn out and holey. But how much of my life ever fits?

Because my socks were baggy and I was usually running around full speed to get somewhere, I would lose my keys and change and wrestling card about as often as I would sweat. They would fall out somewhere, sometime during the day, and I'd have to spend time backtracking to find them, or lose them forever.

My entire existence was like that of a nomad, wandering through the Arizona desert, bumming rides and food, living from wrestling room to wrestling room, Maryvale High, Townsend Saunders, Arizona State, with occasional stops at home for the occasional bit of homework and to see my family. I was always on the move.

So, as difficult as it might be for Patricia Miranda to wrestle me, it was even harder for Tracy to track me down and get me over to the gym to wrestle her on a consistent basis. The problem with wrestling high school kids is that they're, in the end, still high school kids and hard to get in line.

At that time, my life was typified by a certain three hours I spent sitting on the front lawn of our apartment complex. Tracy had dropped me off after wrestling practice, then driven away before I realized I had lost my keys. I reached into the other sock and pulled out my cell phone, which I had stowed there earlier, only to discover that it had been disconnected because we didn't pay the bill.

I had no change for a pay phone, and I didn't know any of the neighbors because transient families rarely know the neighbors, so I couldn't just go up and knock on anyone's door to ask for help. So I just sat on the lawn there and waited for someone to come home to rescue me. And waited. And waited.

While I was waiting, I remember seeing some gang members walk past me, and I remember thinking how easy it would be to hang out with those guys, just get up and go join those guys, go someplace stable, with somebody who cares, a home. But as soon as those thoughts would turn serious, Tracy would somehow always show up to take care of me and I would remember what I was doing and shake myself out of it.

"Where have you been? I've been looking for you for . . ." Tracy would say.

"Just shut up and drive, dude," I would say, grinning, safe at last.

Pretty soon, I started staying four nights a week at Tracy's house, because it was just easier. I loved his wife. And when they later had a child, I bonded with his young daughter. My family wondered what he was doing with me, and I'm sure they thought of him as some strange, older, non-Mexican guy who was trying to take advantage of me, but that wasn't the case at all. He never asked for anything. He never tried to sell any part of me. He wouldn't even try to show off with me, or that he knew me, as he often hung in the back of the room, watching from the corner, never interfering, always there if I needed him.

I think that, as a former wrestling coach running a boring insurance company, he saw me as a chance to be associated with something he loved, while doing something he loved, which was help people. And, man, he saw that I needed help, badly.

He saw that I needed money, that I needed transportation, that I needed a male figure to remind me to shower, tuck in my shirt, be a good kid, and to stop losing my damn keys. He saw that I needed him, and that was enough for him. Some people are just like that, you know? Why do we always have to question those people? Why can't we ever just trust someone? I'm fine with Tracy Greiff being my surrogate father and mentor and friend. In fact, I love it. So why can't everyone else?

In the end, Tracy was able to keep me on schedule and, thus, keep me pointed toward my dream. After spending four days fighting Patricia Miranda the U.S. Olympic officials saw the same things Tracy saw in me. They saw me as a guy with incredible skills, but a guy who was at incredible risk, and an incredible risk to take on. They knew I could one day be an Olympic wrestler. But they also knew that on that same day in a few years, I could be a gangbanger on the street corner. They knew that, for me, the distance between success and failure was the approximate width of a tightrope. They heard about how I lived my daily life, with the crumbling apartments and fast food and constant exposure to the streets, and they knew that I walked that tightrope every day.

They wanted to give me a safety net. They wanted to protect my potential for wrestling greatness—and one of their best young assets—long enough to give me a chance at the Olympics.

So shortly after wrestling Patricia, they started getting the idea that maybe I would be better off living with them, far from where I could get into trouble. Which would mean a move to the Olympic Training Center in Colorado Springs, which was about a fourteen-hour drive from Phoenix.

It was a crazy notion, moving a kid into that intense facility while he was still in high school. But it was something that had been long considered by Doc Bennett, our Olympic wrestling development coach. Doc had been increasingly frustrated by the Olympic wrestling dominance of Eastern European countries, a trend that could be directly tied with the age and experience of their stars.

If you are a great wrestler in Azerbaijan, for example, you are put into a system that grooms you to be an Olympic freestyle wrestler from your early teens. In the United States, as I explained earlier, this system of training begins only after you leave college.

In Azerbaijan, you grow up with freestyle wrestling, the style that is used in the Olympics. In the United States, you grow up with folkstyle wrestling, the style that is used in all the high schools and colleges.

The difference in the two styles is great enough that it takes even the best American wrestlers several years to make the switch and transition successfully. So while a great Azerbaijan wrestler might emerge at age twenty-one, ready to take on the world, the average age of our top wrestlers in international competition here in the United States is twenty-seven.

This gives the Eastern Europeans an obvious advantage as they have a longer wrestling life. They are more skilled, and they are more skilled for longer. So Doc wanted to emulate that training schedule with our system so the U.S. would be more competitive on the international level. The only way to make it happen, however, would be to invite high school kids to live on their own at the Olympic Training Center and start training them in freestyle wrestling earlier than normal.

This country obviously has young ice skaters and gymnasts,

but they all live and train individually near their coaches in various parts of the country. The only person to go into training that early at an Olympic center was speed skater Apolo Anton Ohno, who lived in the winter Olympic Training Center in Lake Placid, N.Y., in the late 1990s. Ohno was an immature kid who initially ditched his flight from Seattle to Lake Placid and disappeared, but eventually he ended up at the center, and eventually it worked out. He wound up winning a gold and silver medal in the 2002 Salt Lake City Olympics, and then won a gold and two bronze medals in the Turin Olympics in 2006.

Using Ohno as a guide, the wise and venerable Doc Bennett wanted to bring me to Colorado Springs to start training as early as possible, and was checking me out from the moment I fought so long and hard with Patricia.

But first, unbeknownst to me at the time, I had to jump through some hoops. Or should I say, pile-drive through some hoops. They wanted to make sure I was serious about this whole wrestling thing.

First, I was invited to spend the summer break after my sophomore year training with Patricia in Colorado Springs. She was preparing for the 2004 Olympics in Athens, Greece, in August, and I could spend that time preparing for my junior year at Maryvale High. This would be sort of a trial run to see if I would like living at the center, and to see if the folks there would like me, and to see if training like this would be successful.

It ended up being a match made in heaven. Or, at least, heaven to me. Walking into the training center that summer for the first time, I thought I was walking into a palace.

It actually looks like this strange military base tucked into the corner of a suburban Colorado Springs neighborhood. It's a collection of low-slung buildings—dorms, athletic facilities, meeting rooms—built around several courtyards. It could be the home of the Colorado National Guard. It's not fancy or glamorous. There are about 140 athletes who live there full-time, and about 350 athletes use the place during the day, all of them coming for serious work and training, the military in sweat suits.

But like I said, to me, it was a palace. My second-floor dorm room was just steps from a shiny dining hall with huge televisions and nice women serving huge portions of food. There were computers in open rooms that we could access at any time. There were machines that spat out rental movies. There was a spectacular view of Pikes Peak from some of the courtyards.

And then, there was my dorm room. Number 332D. Or, as I liked to call it, heaven.

I walked inside and, to the right, there was a huge room with a couch and a desk and I was like, where was the bed? Turns out, that was in a different room, if you can believe it, a separate bedroom on the other side of the living room, and between them there was a separate bathroom. My own bathroom. Are you kidding me? I walked into the bedroom and nearly fainted.

"Tracy, where's my roommates?" I asked.

"You have the room to yourself," he said.

"But, Tracy, who is going to share my bed?"

"You have the bed to yourself."

"Who is going to hog that blanket?"

"It's your blanket."

"Okay, so whose pillow is this?"

"Your pillow."

My pillow? For the first time in my life, I finally had my own pillow, all to myself? I immediately leaped down on the bed and began jumping up and down on it in celebration. It was like some kind of commercial for pillows and I was the happy spokesperson.

"Here's forty bucks, champ. I'll see you in a month," said Tracy.

"I'm rich!" I shouted and kept jumping for joy.

It was quite a month. It may have been the most important month of my life. It was like being at the coolest but most intense summer camp ever. I realized that there was a world outside of my barrio, and in this world, you didn't have to run from dogs to use the bathroom. In this world, you didn't have to fight for food; somebody actually spooned it onto your plate in the world-class cafeteria. In this world, all you had to do was wrestle. This was a place built so you could focus on your sport and how to make yourself better at it—they wanted all other distractions removed, all other worries taken care of, so you could just work at what you did and loved best.

And I embraced that philosophy immediately and fell for it hard. I was so excited, I immediately went to those computers and printed out inspirational sayings from famous people and hung them on my wall.

"We must dare and dare again . . . and go on daring."

"As long as you're going to think anyway, think big."

"Don't wait for your ship to come in, swim out to it."

I think that's what impressed the people in Colorado Springs most during my month there while training with Patricia. As best I could tell, I was the only wrestler who wanted to do nothing but wrestle and grow stronger mentally.

Of course, I also may have been the only wrestler with literally no other distractions: no car, no cell phone, no wallet, and only the forty bucks from Tracy that I carried around in my socks. But still, I took this great opportunity that had been given to me and slammed it to the mat and dang near choked the life out of it.

In the morning, I would get up in my own bed, take off my own blanket, use a sparkling clean bathroom with nobody screaming at me or pounding on the door, run down to a free, healthy breakfast with nobody stealing my food, then go to work with Patricia. Our workouts were a couple of hours, at which point I was free to do whatever else I wanted. But what else could I do?

It was an awesome facility but, at first, I was also the only wrestler without a TV in his room, without a book to his name, without a prayer of ever leaving the facility except on my own two feet, or if someone gave me a ride. And I didn't have the resources to go out to dinner or a movie.

So after I finished wrestling Patricia, I would just keep on wrestling. I would go to the men's wrestling room and go through the long freestyle practice. And then when that was over, I would go through the long Greco-Roman practice. At some point during the day, I would go grab a sandwich and eat it in the wrestling room because, given my young age and my incessant work habits, I didn't have time to make many friends to sit with in the dining hall. So basically, from early morning until late at night, for a solid month, I was in the wrestling room.

When I finally went back to my dorm room, I dropped right into bed, stopping only to scan my only bit of reading material. I found it in one of the drawers in my dorm room when I first got to the Olympic Training Center. Yeah, it was a Bible. Some people read it for inspiration, or for spiritual guidance, but for a month that summer in Colorado Springs, I read it for entertainment. Pretty cool book, once you get into it. I even found the original story my mother was using to compare Angel and me to Cain and Abel. I had no idea those guys really wrestled. Moses wasn't a bad wrestler either, if you think about him fighting with the tablets. And, heck, if Barabbas were alive today, he'd be a headliner on the WWE. There were a lot of struggles in the Bible that I could draw from in my own life.

With all of my wrestling, I figured that the officials here would react in some way. But I had no idea how they would react when they did. It turns out, they phoned Tracy, who relayed the conversation to me like this:

Wrestling Official: "Tracy, we're worried about Henry."

Tracy: "What's wrong?"

Official: "He's going to get hurt."

Tracy: "What's he doing?"

Official: "He's wrestling."

Tracy: "Isn't that what he's supposed to do?"

Official: "He's wrestling *all the time*. He won't leave the wrestling room. He is at every men's and women's practice. All he does is wrestle."

Tracy: "So?"

Official: "It's like the kid is purposely putting himself through some kind of hell."

Tracy: "You don't understand. For Henry, this is heaven."

By the end of that month, they understood. So, too, did the national wrestling community. When I traveled from Colorado

Springs to Fargo, North Dakota, for the junior national championships, I traveled there thanks to Arizona State wrestling, who supported that trip since I had won their tournament the previous year. I had been a two-time state titlist, but now I could see how I matched up with the rest of the country. After all my training, I was excited to have some new competition and to see how I stacked up against other guys my age. The junior national championships were holding tournaments in both freestyle and Greco-Roman wrestling. Since I had been training in both styles in Colorado Springs, I figured I would try both styles in Fargo to see how it would go.

That meant making weight not once, but twice. That meant fighting not seven guys, but fifteen guys. That meant killing myself for three days. Everybody said I was crazy. But to be honest with you, I think I was just hungry. That forty bucks that Tracy "the Philanthropist" Greiff had given me back in Colorado Springs earlier in the summer had long since disappeared. The Olympic folks didn't pay my way when I was on my own at these junior meets. Mostly, I was able to scrape together enough money for plane fare from donations and Tracy, and that was it. I walked into a Fargo gym with no money, no food in my belly, and no idea where I was living after the tournament because the Olympic Training Center was closing down for the Olympics while all the athletes were in Athens competing.

And I feasted. Man, did I feast. I whipped everyone to win the Greco-Roman, then lost a few more pounds and whipped everyone to win the freestyle championships. I was national champion in my weight in two different wrestling styles. I was on top of the world and felt great.

Then, a few days later, I was back in the middle of the desert on the side of the road, alone again.

I had returned to Phoenix after nationals to prepare for my junior season wrestling for Maryvale. There was no homecoming welcome; I returned to a place where I still didn't even have my own bed. There was no publicity, because in the real world, nobody cares about junior wrestling except the junior wrestlers and, usually, their parents. One day, there was even no Tracy, because he had to close some big insurance deal and was off handling that.

So I was riding a borrowed bicycle—at least I don't *think* anyone in my house stole it—on a long trek across town to get to wrestling practice at Arizona State University. I was riding across broken wine bottles and stained hot-dog wrappers and old condoms and the usual stuff that litters poor neighborhoods, the usual stuff that I rode across when, *pop*, the freaking back tire blew out. Who knows what I rode over to puncture it? I just know that my mojo was punctured along with the rubber of my tire. So here I was, a national champion stuck on a busy street in the middle of a Phoenix barrio with no phone and no money and no idea how I was going to get to wrestling practice, which was the only place in this hot desert that I wanted to be.

I could have jogged the ten miles to practice, but my bag was heavy with all my warm-ups and singlets and shoes from the nationals in Fargo. What was I doing with all that stuff? I was going to sell it all at wrestling practice for spending money. I was going to sell all of my memories just to be able to afford Gatorades for a few weeks. Yet on this scorching summer afternoon, fate, and my stupid borrowed bike, wouldn't even allow me to get to where I needed to go to do that.

Having just seen a bit of the outside world in Colorado Springs and gotten a glimpse of other opportunities out there, of an alternate life, and having just whipped the rest of the country in my 112-pound weight class, I was feeling empowered enough at that time to have two thoughts.

1) **My life in Phoenix was a dangerous, potentially destructive mess.**

2) **Dammit, there just had to be another way.**

These thoughts ran through my head as I abandoned the bike by the side of the road and trudged a mile with the heavy bag of wrestling gear thrown over my back to a pay phone to make a collect call to Tracy. By the time I returned to my bike, it was gone. It must've been taken by that rare air-pump-toting bum. By the time Tracy picked me up, I was totally gone mentally, really upset. I had hit the breaking point.

"Dude, this sucks," I told him.

"What sucks?" he asked.

"Here. Me. All of it," I replied.

"Well, you know what doesn't suck?" he said.

"What?" I said.

"This phone call I received today," he said carefully.

I'll never forget this as long as I am breathing and above ground. From the time it took for Tracy's car to drive from one Circle K mini-mart to another Circle K mini-mart—which is about ten seconds in Phoenix—my life entirely changed, the course altered forever.

"Henry, the people in Colorado Springs called," he said.

"Shit, tell them I'll send their Bible back tomorrow," I said.

"They don't want their Bible, they want you," he said.

"But Patricia is going to Athens," I said.

"No, they want you for you. They want you to move up there and live at the Olympic Training Center and start training for 2008 in Beijing."

Me. A high school sophomore. Age seventeen. Being asked to move out of my hellhole, where I'm chased by gangs and poverty and frustration to a paradise where I can chase my dream.

I looked at Tracy and started crying. They were tears of joy at leaving the desert and all that behind. They were tears of fear at the idea and prospect of leaving my family. If I remember correctly, they were mostly tears of hope, something which I never really had let myself feel until that minute, something which right then ran down my face in warm, wonderful trickles.

"Right now," I said firmly.

"Right now?" he said.

"Let's go," I said. "Let's go to Colorado Springs right now. Let's just keep driving until we get there."

"Easy, champ," he said. "We have to stop by home and talk to your mom."

Oh, yeah, her. My mother never paid much attention to my wrestling until I started winning championships; she was too busy trying to keep our family alive. Now that we were growing up, she was trying to keep us together.

Her youngest son moving to Colorado Springs in the middle

of high school was not a good plan if keeping us all together under her eye was the strategy.

Lucky for her, and me, the Olympic officials were also interested in my brother, Angel. Remember him? He is always part of my story, even when he is not a part of my story.

Despite finishing his high school career as probably the greatest high school wrestler in the history of the state of Arizona—unbeaten four-time state champion—Angel was currently mowing lawns. You see, his grades weren't good enough for him to get into college, so he had nowhere to go. The Olympic officials still saw potential in him, though, and still wanted him to come up to Colorado Springs to give it a shot in that new program they were starting.

No, contrary to what everyone thought, we were not a package deal. No, I didn't go up there just to follow Angel. To say that would be a disservice to both of us. The Olympic folks thought he could be a great wrestler. They thought I could be a great wrestler too. They thought it would help that these two kids from this poor neighborhood were brothers and could take care of each other while far from home and everything they were used to.

But we were recruited separately. And, with my mother, because of my age, I had to fight the tougher battle to get her to let me go. No sooner did I tell her about the offer than she became upset and angry. I will translate here as best I can, seeing as it's tough to think and remember in two languages when someone is screaming.

"I knew it; he's kidnapping you!" she cried.

"Who?" I said.

"That Tracy fellow, he's kidnapping you."

"No, Mama, he just took their phone call because I don't have a cell phone."

"Then it's worse!"

"How is it worse?"

"The United States of America is kidnapping you!"

That's what she thought. She was sure I was being kidnapped to be used in some sort of weird weapon test in our war on terror. Like, I don't know, I was going to be strapped to a canister of anthrax and dropped into the mountains of Afghanistan. After all these years of watching her relatives run from the government while always worrying about her own status, she was scared of anything official. She loved America, and she was grateful to America, but sometimes she was scared to death of America.

"This is the Olympics, Mama! This is my dream!" I kept repeating.

She finally relented, and to this day, I don't know why or how I got her to agree to it. I mean, think about it. If your high school son walked home one day and said he had been asked to move by himself to a new town and attend a new high school while living alone in a dormitory with adults who were strangers, what would you say? You would want to talk to the person in charge, right? Now imagine that you can't. Imagine that nobody in this new place speaks your language, so nobody can really tell you what was going on in words you could understand besides your son, who is so eager to go, that you're not sure *what* he is telling you, or if you should believe him. But I was going to be training for the *Olympics*—and that word and that idea is something all people of all languages know and are inspired by. I think that may have helped.

But talk about a leap of faith. My mother allowed her minor son to move eight hundred miles away with no real knowledge of where he was going or what he was going to be doing when he got there. She did it only because he told her this was his dream. I've got to tell you, at that moment, my dream became *our* dream.

As I packed up my stuff—like I said, I wanted to go immediately—I was struck by a couple of things. First, I realized I really didn't have much stuff of my own. Everything I had in the world, all my possessions, they all fit into a tiny souvenir duffel bag. Second, I realized, I really didn't have a choice.

Outside my house was a world filled with long bus rides and broken-down bikes and trouble that was bound to find me sooner or later, the older I got. As I was growing older, many of the tough kids I knew as a child ended up moving back to Mexico and running gangs there, but there were always idiots on my streets, always waiting to get their hands on a local wrestling champ, or any kid. Inside my house was a world that would never get any easier. I couldn't study or concentrate in this nutty environment. I couldn't save any money in this poor household. I couldn't get any better here. I knew there was something else out there for me. I also knew that there were many kids like me who knew about the same opportunities but, because they just weren't good enough or lucky enough, they couldn't do anything about it. I was blessed to not only have a place where I could run, but an opportunity and the ability to run there. I was given not only an escape route, but an escape ticket, and I had to grab it, and grab it now.

I cried again as I hugged my mother goodbye while Tracy waited in the car to drive me up to Colorado Springs. I cried for her strength in letting me go. And I cried for my sadness in that it really wasn't that hard to leave.

My arrival in Colorado Springs for the start of the rest of my life was, in one way, much like my arrival there earlier that summer. Tracy dropped me off and threw me some money. Only this time, his allowance had increased from forty dollars to sixty dollars. And this time, at least for the time being, I would not be living alone.

With the training center dorms closed until after the August Olympics, but with my new school starting in August, I needed a temporary place to stay so I could start school. The good folks at USA Wrestling figured that since I was so used to living around a bunch of people, they would house me with a local family, where I shared a room with two other kids. And maybe because I had stolen that Bible, the USA Wrestling people also thought I was very religious. They must have thought that, because they housed me with a family that prayed about eighteen times a day. Talk about my sins biting me in the butt.

This family was very nice, very hospitable. I owe them a lot. But it felt like I was living on the moon. It was so different from what I had known previously, or even what I had experienced when I had come up for my short stay before at the Olympic Training Center. I was in this house only a couple of months, but it was enough to make me understand the culture shock I was about to endure for the next four years. Nobody here spoke Spanish. Nobody here ate Mexican ice cream. Nobody here fought in the living room over whether to watch *The People's Court* or *Jerry Springer*. Everybody here was just so nice. And I was just so lost. Besides all the praying, there was a lot of sleeping. Way more than I was used to. Everyone in this family went to bed at eight o'clock every night. This was tough on a kid who was used to being a night owl. Back in Arizona, because of the three-hour bus rides to wrestling practice, I often didn't get home until midnight. Being in a normal enviroment was like having jet lag—cultural jet lag. I would be up, alert, ready to go when everyone else was sound asleep down the hall, and it was pretty lonely.

I will never forget how, in the first weeks in my new town, in a place where I had gone to train for the Olympics, I couldn't even watch the Olympics to get inspired. They were on tape delay television from Athens every night for two weeks in August, yet my family was in bed by then, and I had to go to bed with them. Lights out. No TV. No Olympics.

When the Olympics finally ended and they reopened the Olympic Training Center dormitories, I was thrilled for two reasons. First, I would once again, for the second time in my life, get my own bed in my own room. And, second, Angel would now be joining me. I had gone up early to start school, but he had already graduated and didn't have those same restraints and now he was coming up to live at the training center.

I know it sounds crazy, but that first night Angel was there, I felt more alone than I had ever felt in my life. My own brother was down the hall, and here I was in my own little room by myself. I couldn't hear him. I couldn't see him if I rolled over and opened my eyes. I couldn't punch him in the ribs when he tried to steal my pillow. He was so close but so far away. What happened next is something out of a Disney movie, but what can I say, sometimes I've got the heart of a little stuffed animal.

In the middle of the night, on my first permanent night staying in room 332D at the Olympic Training Center after moving in earlier that day from the local family's house, I shuffled down the hall and knocked on the door of my brother's room.

"Angel, you in there?" I whispered.

"Where the hell else would I be?" he answered.

"Angel, can I come in?" I asked.

"What for?" he said.

"Just because," I said.

And so it happened that for the first week of my permanent stay in my dream home with my own bed and my own pillow and my own covers, I slept on the cold, hard floor with my brother. We huddled under the same kind of blankets that for years had been our only furniture and our only comfort. We arched our backs against the kind of floor that for years had been our only resting place. What can I say? It was what we were used to, and being out of place, we naturally tried to find something familiar, some way of remembering where we came from, even as we were trying to forget it.

It was as if, before starting our new life, we had to soak in the last ounces of strength from our old one. We stared out the window at the foreign landscape and then stared at each other and huddled under the covers.

"Angel, you scared?" I whispered, even though nobody was listening.

"Nah," he said.

A few moments later, he nudged me.

"Henry, you scared?" he said.

"Nah," I said.

With that, the two tough hombres from the barrio fell fitfully asleep in the suburbs. A wrestling mat only yards away that was going to be our ultimate test.

We had traveled to the farthest reaches of our imaginations. And we were about to travel even farther.

★ SIX ★

I still remember the first bite of the first free food, the first sting of the first large, luxurious shower, the first flush of the first unclogged toilet, the first softness of the first real, fluffy pillow, the first long, easy stretch of my arms into the first uncrowded spaces of my life.

I still remember that first morning I awoke in my own Colorado Springs dorm room, looked outside my own window, and saw heaven, or at least pine trees and a courtyard and the windows of the dining hall, which was pretty damn close to heaven.

"This is Disneyland!" I shouted.

I was right, but in more ways than I could imagine, and not all of them in the good way that I first imagined.

Yes, beginning in that fall of 2004, my life at the U.S. Olympic Training Center as a high school junior was about amazing sights and exciting experiences, Flying Teacups and long sweet churros. But my life was also about the scary rides. It was also about the Thunder Railroads and Space Mountains. The roller coasters that were terrifying as much as they were thrilling.

For every neat, new, exciting moment I would spend in the wrestling room or dining hall, I would spend an uncomfortable, awkward, strange moment outside the center. While I was a high school wrestling prodigy working toward his goal of one day being in the Olympics, I was also a poor Mexican-American kid living on his own in a strange land, a new state, a new school, far from his family and the familiarity of his normal wrestling room and coach. It was wonderful. And it was weird. It was scary.

Let's start with my new high school. Coronado High School in suburban Colorado Springs. I won two state wrestling championships for them and am proud to be an alumnus, even though sometimes it felt like I was barely there.

Part of the promise made by the Olympic officials to convince my mother to let me come to Colorado Springs was that I would attend and graduate high school. But they never said which high school. And they never promised it would be easy. And it wasn't; no, it definitely was not.

First, there were the students. To me, they all seemed rich. By rich I mean that they wore clothes with nice labels and drove cars that were their own and that didn't chug and smoke. I would show up every day in old T-shirts and even older sweatpants, looking like some trespassing bum. The district school that I should've gone to was Palmer High School, since I was living at the Olympic Training Center. But I ended up at Coronado instead since they had a great wrestling team. I was picked up from the Olympic Training Center most mornings by Mrs. Cooper, the counselor at Coronado, but I would usually find my own way home on my bike which I would stuff into her car each morning I rode with her. It was an unusual arrangement.

Second, there was the students' skin color. To me, they were all white, which, I guess, in my mind, is part of why I thought they were all rich. I had always assumed that white people were wealthy, or at least, wealthier than I was. With my dark complexion, I looked like some lost child of the school's gardeners.

Third, there was the students' language and way of talking. From locker to lunch room, everyone spoke what seemed like a very exact, proper, grammatical brand of English. With my Ebonics Spanglish, I sounded like a gang member.

So, no, I didn't exactly fit in. It certainly didn't help that my manic wrestling schedule made it impossible to fit in, that my whole life revolved around getting into the wrestling room as much as possible. My schedule then was that I would wake up at four thirty a.m., endure a wrestling workout at the training center at five a.m., then somehow find a way to leave for school by seven. I would take classes until about twelve thirty p.m.; then I would return to the center for wrestling practice at two p.m., after lunch. I would then spend the rest of the afternoon in the wrestling room, do a little homework in my dorm room at night, then pass out, dead tired and bone exhausted, at about ten p.m.

As you can see, this didn't leave much time for making friends or socializing. Okay, I'll be honest. I had no friends. I was this short, weird-looking, odd-sounding kid who just didn't fit in and wasn't from around there, and was obsessed with wrestling. I would go from class to class in the morning without talking to anyone, the only kid from the training center at the high school, once again a newbie and an outcast, silently going through the motions of being a student. Then at lunchtime I would sit and eat with the teachers. They knew I was alone, so they would let me hang out in their lounge with them for company. Even when I started wrestling with the Coronado High team, I still had no friends, except for one volunteer coach, the one guy in about one hundred square miles who spoke my language, and got me, was interested in me for me.

His name was Dave Hurtado, and after about five days of watching me walk silently around the halls of the school with my head down, he realized that maybe I was looking to run into someone like him.

"So, do you like it here?" he stopped and asked me one day.

"It's Disneyland!" I said.

"Really?" he said.

Pause.

"Um, can I come over for dinner?" I said. It seemed all I needed was for one person to say a kind word to me and I was their friend.

Mr. Hurtado was a warm family man who somehow knew exactly how I felt, far from home and in a place where I didn't know anyone. When we weren't eating at his house, he would take me out to restaurants, buy me dinner, talk to me about school, just spend time with me and listen to what I had to say. Once he even drove Angel and me to the fancy Broadmoor hotel for an afternoon of swimming at the hotel pool. It was the strangest experience. Paying people to park your car? Paying people to open the front door for you? Hell, there were many times in my life when I had access to neither a car nor a front door, much less being able to pay anyone to handle them and take care of them!

My brother and I were both so uncomfortable around so much privilege, we were afraid to strip down to our bathing suits, nervous that everyone would stare at our strange brown bodies.

"Lesson number one," said Mr. Hurtado. "No matter where you go in your life, you have to act like you own the place."

So we changed into our suits and walked to the huge pool and . . . no way. I mean, no way. That strange-smelling chemical water? Those half-naked white people? Everyone looking at Angel and me like they wanted us to bring them another fresh towel or a drink? We may have owned the place, but we were selling the mysterious pool, and all the anxiety it brought with it, as soon as we could.

"You guys," said Mr. Hurtado, shaking his head. "I can't take you anywhere."

Especially since we'd been nowhere.

I had no trouble, however, making myself at home at Mr. Hurtado's house, both Angel and me descending upon them and soaking in their hospitality. Soon I was spending a couple of days a week there, sometimes just curling up on his couch watching TV in wonder. I was amazed not at the couch, but the TV, which was not fuzzy, not affixed with a clothes hanger, nor the object of a fistfight. His house was a safe place for me, a comfortable place.

During the commercials we talked about a lot of stuff, especially school, which I was conquering academically in the classroom, if not socially. I even made my first honor roll in my first semester at Coronado because I had nothing else to do but study and listen. Besides wrestling, of course.

We also talked about high school wrestling, which, frankly, was a joke for me at that point. Other wrestlers looked at me as if I were Michael Jordan playing on their intramural basketball team. They seemed to cower the minute I walked into the wrestling room, and no one wanted to wrestle and get on the mat with me. This made it hard to get good workouts with the high school team, but even harder during matches, because lots of kids flat-out wouldn't want to fight me. I would approach them on the mat, lift one hand and—boom—they would fall and curl up and be done. I would stand there, shrug, and fall on them, but never without whispering in their ear, "C'mon, I'll let you up if you'll just fight me. C'mon, it's not so bad." Not once did any of them take me up on the offer.

Mr. Hurtado and I also talked about life, which, on February 9, 2005, suddenly got a lot better and a lot brighter. That was the day that, at age eighteen, I had my first honest-to-goodness birthday party thrown for me by Mr. Hurtado. This included my first birthday cake, a sweet pretty little chocolate thing with a Mexican flag on it. Some other wrestlers from the training center showed up. I don't know if they came to honor me, or just to gawk at me as I floated around the room with my eyes as big as saucers and a wide grin plastered on my face. For the first time ever, I was honored with birthday candles that I got to make a wish on and blow out. And for the first time ever, a bunch of people sang me the birthday song. All these years, when thinking about all the birthdays we never celebrated, all those birthdays for Angel and Gloria and all my siblings and me that just slipped by, I wondered why it was such a big deal. Well, that day I finally found out.

A kid who was never given five minutes to shine for something other than wrestling suddenly was granted an entire day. A kid who used to go to sleep by candlelight was suddenly blowing them out for fun and to make a wish come true.

Yes, life was getting better and better and soon I hit the jackpot. At age eighteen, I not only learned how to drive, but I was given a car.

Now don't go thinking that suddenly I was in the lap of luxury. This car was no luxury; it was a last-minute necessity caused by the following late-February phone conversation with my mentor, Tracy Greiff.

"Tracy, it's Henry," I said.

"Hey, what's up?" he said.

"Tracy, I just rode my bike home from school."

"So? You do that every day."

"Tracy, it took me nearly two hours today."

"What happened? Did you crash?"

"Tracy, have you checked the weather up here?"

Tracy being in Arizona, where it never snows and wintry weather is rare, had no idea that it was freezing and snowing in Colorado Springs, although he should have known, because it was *always* freezing and snowing there. Or even worse, blizzarding, as it had been that day.

"Tracy, have you ever tried riding a bike through a blizzard? Have you ever tried riding a bike on ice? Have you ever tried going to school after that?"

Being the loving, caring philanthropist that he is, Tracy paused for the longest time, thinking it all over, coming up with a plan like he always does.

"All right, all right," he said. "I'll get you a car."

He paused.

"Wait a minute," he said. "You don't know how to drive one!"

This is where Mr. Hurtado entered the picture in the whole car plan. Being my Colorado Springs guardian angel, he took me to a grade school parking lot across from his house and taught me how to drive. For the first three lessons, I kept going in circles. I couldn't concentrate on the road. I still can't. Folks say I'm still a terrible driver, my mind being too focused on my wrestling and everything else racing through my head, unable to share mental space with thoughts of other drivers and cars on the road with me.

But thanks to Mr. Hurtado and those parking lot sessions, I did get my license. And Tracy did arrange for me to buy a used Saab with over 100,000 miles on it. Like I said, he's quite the philanthropist. Hey, in the first couple of months, I only wrecked it once. How was I supposed to know that you're supposed to put on the parking brake when parking on a hill? I've never run faster than when I chased that rolling Saab down the hill. I've never cursed louder than when I couldn't catch it before it smacked into a pole.

But, bless my heart, little Henry Cejudo was growing up. He had shelter, food, a car to get around in, a dream, and a place to chase that dream. Now all he really needed was one more thing to make this picture of arrested adolescence complete.

Cover your eyes. Close your ears. This is the part where I write about my first girlfriend.

Her name is Clarissa Chun. Some would call her drop-dead gorgeous. I prefer to call her pile-driver beautiful, using wrestling terms. You see, before we ever held hands, we shared half-nelsons. You guessed it. Like Patricia Miranda, Clarissa Chun is a female wrestler.

Where else was I going to meet a woman? How else could I have actually held a conversation with a woman? I lived in the wrestling room and it was what I knew best, so it was quite predictable that my first girlfriend would come from that room. Weird, sort of sketchy, but definitely predictable.

I first saw her in the summer of 2004, when I was working with Patricia. No, I wasn't her workout partner. But yes, after checking her out, I really wanted to be.

Understand, at that point in my life, at age seventeen, I had not yet even been on a date. It wasn't that I was small and ugly and uncouth, although, sure, maybe some people felt that way. It was that I was so involved in wrestling, I didn't have time for anything else. And I didn't meet anyone, really, who wasn't involved in wrestling too.

And we were so poor, I didn't have the money for anything else. At age seventeen I had never been to a dance, never been to the movies with a group of kids that included girls, never been to a girl's house for a party, nothing. If I was going to meet someone, it would have to be in a wrestling room, which pretty much eliminated most women on the face of this earth.

Ah, but not Clarissa. I noticed her immediately. You would, too. Beautiful eyes, high cheekbones, silken hair, killer body. Well, of course she had a killer body. It sort of goes without saying that if you are a future world champion wrestler at 105 pounds, you will have a killer body. Given her strength, it was literally a killer body.

I was also attracted to another aspect—her age. She was twenty-three. She was an older woman. Okay, so she was only five-and-a-half years older than me, but when you are seventeen, that is like five hundred years older. To the rest of the world, she was a kitten, but to me, she was a wildcat—smart and sleek and sexy as hell.

I first noticed her one day when I was thrown to my back by Patricia. I was thrown to my back because I had just spotted Clarissa and I was distracted—I couldn't tear my eyes away. She had somebody in a leg lock on the next mat, and, man, she had some awesome legs. I know, it's strange to be checking out a woman while you are wrestling another woman, but, hey, are there really any rules to a social life as whacked out as this?

It was only a matter of time before I made my move. Well, it was sort of a move.

"Hey, Clarissa, I'm Henry Cejudo," I said.

"Hey, Henry," she said.

"You wanna wrestle?" I said.

I was actually serious about the wrestling part. Clarissa was about the same size as Patricia, so I knew I could help her. Wrestling with her, for me, was like another couple taking a walk through the park on their first date. For us, it was a normal and natural way to begin things. It wasn't until we had worked out a couple of times, after teaching her all sorts of new wrestling moves, that I made my first real move. It was after a workout. We were sitting side by side on a bench in the wrestling room, sweating, red-faced, and out of breath, when I turned and gave her the only opening line I knew.

"You want my wrestling shoes?" I said.

"Your what?" she said.

"Here, I've got these nice Adidas shoes. I'll put in some insoles, they'll fit you perfect. You really need a pair like this."

Up to that point in my life, whenever somebody wanted to curry my favor, they gave me clothes or free stuff. I figured I would do the same with Clarissa to get her attention. I took off one of my shoes and handed it to her. It was then I noticed that all the tread was worn down and that the shoes sort of, well, stunk.

"Henry, this is nice, but I already have shoes," she said.

"Not like these," I said, my confidence wilting by the minute.

"No, you're right, not like those," she said with a warm smile.

She didn't take my shoes. But damn, she grabbed my heart. We started working out less and hanging out more. By hanging out, I mean, we would grab a drink of water together between the men's and women's workout. I might walk her out to her truck afterward, small talk, a few laughs, nothing serious.

It was the winter of my first year there in Colorado Springs, and I would have gone farther faster, but I was lonely and she was lovely. And I had one major problem that you may have already noticed. I had no idea what the hell I was doing when it came to a girlfriend. I didn't know how to talk to women. About the only thing I had ever seriously said to a woman was "Nice move" while rolling around with her on a wrestling mat. The only other women in my life had been my mother, who talked with me mostly about God, and my sisters, who could never be heard because of all the household screaming.

I needed help. I needed a Cyrano. I needed my man Eric. His name is Eric Albarracin, he's a fellow wrestler and one of my first friends in Colorado Springs. He was in his early thirties, a former army captain who was wise in the ways of the world and the ways of women. One of the first times he saw me in the dorm, he put his hand on my shoulder and stared into my eyes.

"Dude, I've seen young ones like you come through here and get broken in half," he said. "I'm tired of being the one to pick up the pieces."

"Nobody's breaking me," I said confidently.

"Oh yeah?" he said.

Little did I know that not only would I be broken, but the first person to break me was going to be a woman. I finally came to Eric when I realized I was facedown, pinned, with nowhere to move.

"You need to help me talk to this girl," I said.

"Here, give me your phone," he said.

And with that, the courtship of Clarissa Chun began. It was through the words and fingers of Eric Albarracin. He would text her pretending to be me.

"Hey there," said one text. "You ready to take a chance on me?"

"Hey there," said another text. "You better come watch me wrestle tonight at the high school. Maybe I'll let you take me out later."

"Hey you," said yet another, bolder text. "You ready to get lucky?"

The lucky one, of course, was me. Clarissa was charmed by the texts. She thought I was cute and funny and sweet, and she actually came out to one of my high school meets to cheer me on, and afterward we had our first date. At least, I think it was a date.

She bought me dinner at a family restaurant. She had money, and I still didn't even have a wallet.

It was love at first quesadilla. For the first time in my life, I was with someone who cared about only me.

She cared about my appearance and fixed me up. We would go shopping and she would pick out nice clothes and buy them for me. She was teaching me to look less like a Mexican gang-banger and more like a normal teenager.

She cared how I lived. She would constantly remind me that discarded orange and banana peels should not be left on coffee tables. Water bottles should not be allowed to collect in the corners. Napkins should not be shredded on the ground and left there. When she worked on me to pick up my clothes, I told her that this was the first time I had owned any extra clothes—how was I supposed to know to hang them up when I wasn't wearing them? She didn't buy that.

Most important, she cared how I felt. When I was down, she would let me stay at her house, talking to me all through the night. When I was lonely for home, she would hug me. When I was feeling like an outcast at school, she would say something to make me laugh and lift my spirits.

I loved her like I had never loved anyone. And, of course, I didn't care that I was seventeen and she was twenty-three. I didn't care that we had to sneak around because we thought people wouldn't approve of our age difference. I didn't care that we would have to drive thirty minutes away so we could have dinner without anyone seeing us. I didn't care about anything but being with her and spending time with her.

Even though, as you may have also guessed by now, I really didn't know how to be with her, if you know what I mean. I was as lost at intimacy as I was at a country club swimming pool. This is where Eric Albarracin came in again.

Once I turned eighteen, I wanted to be closer to Clarissa and I felt like it was time to make the next move, but I had no idea what to do. This time, Eric would use his own phone and text me what to do, instructions on how to woo Clarissa. I would be sitting with Clarissa on the couch and he would literally text me and tell me what to do next.

Eventually, I figured it out, though. I muddled through until I got it right. Eventually, well, imagine the contortions of world-class wrestlers on a mat. Now imagine those contortions occurring on a bed. Out of respect for Clarissa, I won't describe it any further. But out of respect for the truth . . . wow!

Clarissa had just broken up with another wrestler, though, a guy in my weight class named Stephen Abas (the guy I would eventually go on to defeat to qualify for the Olympics), and she announced to me that she would never go through the drama of dating another wrestler. But six months after she made this statement, we essentially moved in together. Well, okay, she had the apartment and all the stuff, so I actually moved in with her.

She said she loved my dedication to wrestling and my family. She said she loved my innocent sweetness.

I told her I loved her beauty and her strength. I told her I loved how she really took care of me, how she was my sugar mama and my sweet mama and my hot mama all rolled into one.

But I was one of the only ones. As you can imagine, my family was not thrilled that I had a girlfriend, especially one who was older than I was. And eventually I didn't blame them, though at the time I ignored their advice.

The closer I grew to Clarissa, the more I neglected the

stuff that should have been important to me at that point in my wrestling career. Yeah, my first love was eventually becoming the first thing to hurt my future. The future I'd worked so hard for.

Remember how I made the honor roll in my first semester at Coronado? Then, in February of that year, I won the Colorado State 119-pound wrestling championship against Billy Wright of Loveland High. I beat him 22–7; it wasn't even close. This being my third consecutive state title, but my first in a different state, I was starting to actually get my name in the newspaper. And other wrestlers were actually beginning to be quoted about me.

Listen to this quote from Wright: "He caught me off guard. I've never seen anybody do that. There was nothing I could do."

There was "nothing he could do." Dude said a mouthful of truth. Pretty cool, huh? I was so excited I gave my medal to Mr. Hurtado like I was giving him real gold. I wanted him to feel as rich as he had made me feel. The new attention was heady stuff for a long-ignored kid. It put a new strut in my step and a bulge in my chest.

Then Clarissa came into the picture. We started dating soon after that championship. And pretty soon, I was feeling good enough about her to let her completely into my life while shutting everything and everyone else out.

This started with school. By the time I had reached my senior year, I was sick of it. I was sick of driving there in the dark in the snow, already tired from wrestling practice, all just to spend a morning hanging out with strangers. Yeah, the people there were still strangers. A tiny brown wrestling champion doesn't exactly equal a cool kid in any school, does it? I was sick of eating lunch with the teachers. I was sick of feeling the white kids staring at me. I was sick of everyone talking about going to

My mother, my father, and me at the beach. I had weird blond hair
as a little kid.

Me and my dad, looking strong.

My mother holding my brother George, Gloria and Angel on the couch. That's my sister Barbara holding on to me and Alonzo sitting on the floor with us. We're in our house in South Central, L.A.

Angel, a friend, me, and George acting up.

Angel and I (with the Mohawk) playing around in the dirt lot that was our front lawn in New Mexico. I think he had just finished beating me up.

Tracy and I hang out at the USA Olympic Training Center in Colorado Springs in 2004 when I first arrived there.

Playing around at the Olympic Training Center in 2004.

It wasn't all fun and games, though, in Colorado. Here's a typical day in the training room. I'm in the middle, and I'm being trained by Sergei Beloglazov, two-time Olympic gold medalist and legendary wrestler.

I had a ton of great supporters in Beijing, including (*from left to right*) Jeffrey Lopez, Angela Delgado, Tracy Greiff, Gloria Cejudo, Frank Saenz, David Hurtado, Jesse Abarca, Alonzo Cruz, and Angelica Montero.

I had terrific coaches at the Olympics. Here Kevin Jackson (*left*) and Terry Brands (*center*) and I discuss strategy.

I had to defeat Radoslov Velikov of Bulgaria (the 2006 world champion) in the first match. I'm doing a gut wrench move here.

In my second match, I faced Besarion Gochashvili from Georgia. I won the quarterfinals here.

My semifinal match was against Namig Sevdimov from Azerbaijan.

The finals were against Tomohiro Matsunaga of Japan. It took me nine seconds to win the second round and clinch the gold with a great high-crotch takedown.

I was overwhelmed when I knew I had won the gold medal for the USA. Kevin Jackson and Terry Brands were elated.

PHOTO BY LARRY SLATER

It was one of the proudest moments of my life, standing on the podium, accepting the gold medal.

Look at these guys eyeing my medal! With my fellow medalists: Tomohiro Matsunaga (silver), and Radoslav Velikov and Besik Kudukhov (both bronze).

PHOTO BY LARRY SLATER

Me with the medal and flag and family and friends in front of
The Tonight Show with Jay Leno.

Me and Mom at *The Tonight Show* with Jay Leno, after winning the gold.

college when I would just be going back to the Olympic Training Center. I didn't care about college. I took recruiting trips to a couple of big places but only because I wanted to get out of town for the weekend. College wasn't my answer, and I was sick of everyone talking about it like it was the only answer.

I tried to be different and stand out in my senior year by wearing a suit to school every day, just to show people that I wasn't the gardener's son, that I wasn't some gaucho who had just walked across the river. Even that didn't work. The school held a fashion show, I entered, and even in my blue blazer and red tie, I lost to all the popular boys, and it made me furious.

I stopped studying and soon I just stopped showing up to school at all. I started missing so many classes, Mr. Hurtado actually had to sometimes drag me to school and physically take me to the classroom and wait outside so I wouldn't escape. I was flunking out, and I didn't care. I was making myself more of an outcast, and it didn't matter to me.

"This damn place sucks. This crappy life sucks. I'm going back to Arizona," I complained as I was scraping ice off my car, parked one morning in Mr. Hurtado's driveway.

"You're lucky I'm not your real father," said Hurtado. "If I was, you would not be wrestling anymore. You are letting yourself down. You are blowing your chances."

I stopped scraping. I rubbed the ice chips out of my eyes, their cold replaced with a warmth that felt like tears.

Mr. Hurtado talked as if he were my father. Nobody in Colorado Springs had done that before. Nobody had ever tried to take my father's place or speak to me fatherly words of wisdom. I wept for my father's loss and for my loss of my father, and for Mr. Hurtado's love. I hugged him and promised to be better.

If only I had been mature enough then to keep that promise.

It was three days before the state wrestling tournament in my senior season. I was in physical education class with this idiot from our school basketball team. He was the star and a big man on campus, and I think it always bothered him that I didn't recognize him as such. In fact, I barely even talked to him at all. So he started making fun of me, all the usual stuff—my size, my skin color, all the idiot stuff.

"You better stop," I told him.

"Who's going to make me?" said the idiot.

"I'm telling you, you better stop," I told me.

"You stop me," said the idiot.

So I did. Bam! Did I ever. Bam! Bam! With three jabs, I punched him out, knocked him down, made him woozy, and promised to finish the job after school. I know, I'm a wrestler, I'm not supposed to be able to throw fists, but just feel a wrestler's arm sometime. You'll realize that it's not about the fists; it's about the power behind them.

Later that day, waiting on a field for this bozo to come finish the fight, along with a bunch of kids who had come to watch, I noticed a familiar car drive up. It was Mr. Hurtado. He climbed out and ran up to me in a fury.

"What are you thinking?" he said. "You hurt this kid, your career is over! You can't hit people! You can't fight people! What is wrong with you?"

What was wrong with me was that, at a stunted age eighteen, I had blossomed into a full-grown rebellious teenager. I didn't hug Mr. Hurtado that time. I just kept waiting for this kid to show up, my prey. But then I got lucky. Twice.

First, I got lucky because the basketball star never showed

up, thus keeping me out of another fight and probably out of jail. Second, the school officials suspended me for only one day, allowing me to still compete in that state tournament in two days.

On that Wednesday I stayed home for suspension, and on Thursday I showed up for the tourney, fully eligible and really angry and fired up. This time, the final match was a 24–7 victory over a kid named Ty Bennett. Once again, it wasn't even close. And once again, having completed a 25–0 regular season with a fourth consecutive state championship spanning two states, the public praise for my wrestling skills started flowing.

"It would take a miracle for someone to beat him," said Tony George of Wasson High.

More than that, by now it would take a miracle for me to think I could do anything wrong on the wrestling mat. In the spring and summer of 2005, I grew even closer to Clarissa while shutting down other parts of my life. First my school, then my family. They were worried about me spending so much time with Clarissa. They were concerned that it was hurting my wrestling. My national coach, Terry Brands, had already complained to them about it. They were going to do something about it.

Angel was busy with his own wrestling, so the rest of my family had to pitch in and set me straight. One afternoon that spring before nationals, Alonzo and my mom suddenly showed up, knocking on the door to my dormitory room. I wasn't there, of course. Hell, I was never there. I was living with Clarissa, remember?

Even though they had just flown in from Arizona, they were more angry than tired, so they sat down outside my room and waited. And waited. And waited. When I finally showed up to pick up some clothes, they knew where I had been. They ushered me into my dorm room. My mom sat on the bed. And my brother jumped right in my face. Warning: The following quotations are crude, but they're real.

"Dude, you've accomplished so many things, and now you're going to let this girl screw your shit up!" Alonzo screamed. "If she messes up, she has a safety net. You don't! I know you think it's cool to hang out with an older chick, but stop it, now!"

I quietly hugged my brother. I quietly hugged my mother. Then I quietly walked away.

I loved this girl, dammit. Nobody had ever kissed me, but she kissed me. Nobody ever hugged me, but she hugged me. I didn't care what anyone said. I loved this girl, and I was focused on her and not the advice from my family.

And, at least for the moment, she was still not affecting my wrestling performance. I was the high school state champion in February; then, in the spring, I became the first high school kid to ever win a national senior championship, which is a tournament featuring every great wrestler of every age, a tournament whose champions were usually guys in their late twenties.

I was on top of the world. I felt like I couldn't be beaten. Who needed high school? Who needed my family?

My senior year ended and I blew off everything. I skipped the prom because of a wrestling practice. I didn't show up for graduation because I was at the world team trials, where I finished second. Two years at Coronado, and I didn't attend one extracurricular activity that didn't involve me or wrestling. Not one football game. Not one basketball game. Not one dance. Two years after I enrolled, they mailed me my degree and sent me out into a world where I had already been living by myself. I hated

Coronado. Or did I hate it that I was never stable enough to love Coronado? That I never had that typical high school experience? I could never figure that out.

Either way, it was two summers before the Olympics and I was certain I was headed for greatness and a final realization of the dream I had been working toward ever since I had announced it from that milk crate—a gold medal. So life was going okay. Hell, I even had some money in my pocket. Because my Olympic dream would be stunted by college—even though I was recruited by every great program in the country—I could finally accept tournament money. For winning nationals and the Pan-Am Games that spring and summer, I received four thousand dollars, which felt like four million to me.

I was on easy street. Initially I had a part-time job of cleaning up abandoned houses for extra cash. But after graduation, I immediately quit. I then moved in completely with Clarissa and acted like her young husband.

Who needed high school? Who needed haughty family members who I thought didn't understand me or what I wanted, what was best for me? Who needed . . . wrestling?

Ooops. You figured it had to happen sooner or later. Having turned my back on two of the three most important things in my life, you had to figure that it would eventually be a clean sweep and I would fall tumbling back to earth.

The softness of Clarissa made me tired of the roughness of wrestling. And my growing empowerment made me tired of the toughness of my nationals coach, Terry Brands.

Terry is a former national champion and legendary wrestling figure. His weight class was 126 pounds, but he himself had the intensity of a giant. He won three national titles, two world titles, and a bronze medal at the 2000 Olympics in Sydney. By the way, he had earlier named a daughter after the city, as if it would help motivate him. Sydney. I'm serious. This guy was that intense. And totally committed to wrestling.

He was happy to have me join his team in Colorado Springs. He even changed the entire training schedule so I could fit in my high school classes and graduate. I'll never forget him for that, and will always be grateful. But I'll also never forget him for how hard he worked us. He forced me to be a man before I was physically ready. Not too many people can survive Terry Brands as a coach. I barely did.

Once, he woke up the entire team at three a.m. to run Colorado Springs' famed Manitou Incline, a 3.25-mile uphill trail over abandoned railroad tracks. It was dark, and snowing, and it didn't matter. We were slipping and falling, flailing in the dark, and it didn't matter. By the end, most of us were crawling and cursing, and he was just shrugging. We finished that climb just in time for me to return to my dorm, eat breakfast, and go to school. Now you see why I sometimes had trouble showing up for class with my full attention?

Terry would say he was trying to make us strong. But many of us thought he was only trying to make us hurt. Or to break us.

Then there were the times he would turn up the sauna to about two hundred degrees and order every wrestler on the team to stand inside. Once we were all packed in there, he closed the door and stood outside and refused to let us leave.

There were, like, fifty guys enclosed in that smothering sauna, all crammed together naked. We couldn't sit down, we wouldn't get out, and grown men would start freaking out and crying. It was fifty nasty breaths on your face, and fifty globs of sweat rubbing against you in the heat.

The first guy to lose his mind and force his way out would be the weakest link. The last guy to stay was the strongest. All of us would stay at least an hour before the carnage would begin. My own personal best finish in the sauna test was third from the last. I was next to a heavyweight who could sweat more than I could and had more weight to lose, and a middleweight who was into some kind of weird meditation and could zone out all the angst around him and mentally power through to victory. I finally left the sauna when I started hallucinating. I saw clouds. I saw heaven. I fell into hell. I was seventeen years old. Ask my coach—he will confirm every word of this. He knew what he was doing, even if we had no idea. That bastard Terry Brands.

In the end I liked him because his approach worked for me. But often I wondered if it was worth it. Like the time he made me to go the weight room and curl every dumbbell from ten pounds to one hundred pounds, each one in sets of ten. That was the day that, after arriving at school, I couldn't do any work because I couldn't lift my arms. They were totally dead—I couldn't even pick up a pen to take notes with. That bastard Terry Brands.

He would make us call him if we were going to be late for practice. He would make us tuck in our shirts when we were outside the wrestling room. It was very military. He had us all in chains and forward march.

Appropriately, perhaps, this was also the year I almost died. After surviving some of the toughest neighborhoods in the United States, I nearly died in one of the prettiest spots on earth.

It was the spring of 2006, I had just won a gold medal in the Pan American championships in Rio de Janeiro, and I headed for the famed Copacabana Beach to celebrate. The waves were so high, red flags were everywhere, but, hey, no problem. I had just ridden several of the toughest wrestlers in the world. I couldn't ride a little wave?

Well, actually, no. Moments after I swam away from shore, I was engulfed in salt water and spray and foam and fear. The waves were much higher than they looked from shore, and I was much smaller than I seemed on a wrestling mat, and before I knew it, I was drowning. Literally drowning. My arms and legs were twisted from the shock of the waves and cramping from the fright of the situation. I could only keep my head above water for a few moments at a time. I was swallowing water and sinking lower and suddenly I was looking at the face of my mother. I could see her crying. I could see me dying. This was how it would end. God let me climb so high, but I wasn't going to climb any higher.

Then I felt His hand. Actually, it wasn't His hand; it was the hand of a surfer, grabbing my arm and pulling me above the foam. Then I felt another hand, of another surfer, grabbing my leg and putting me on a board.

Where I was once fighting death below the waves, now I was clinging to life above them, hanging on to the surfboard as water crashed around us, trying to clear my lungs as we lunged to shore.

When we finally reached the sand, I kissed it and rolled in it and lay there while water kept spewing from my mouth. When I finally looked up, several hundred beachgoers were glaring at me from beyond the red flags while my two rescuers were standing above me, shaking their heads and cursing at me in Portuguese.

What can I say? It was that kind of horrible year. In the summer of 2006, I finally had had enough. I started doing something I had never done before. I started backing off and slacking off. I missed some wrestling practices. I blew off some conditioning drills. I was no longer living my sport in the wrestling room. Mostly it was because I was too busy living my love with Clarissa.

Terry knew I was giving less than the 1,000 percent that I usually gave. He knew I was actually trying to be normal, to carve out some identity separate from wrestling. But he was trying to turn me into an Olympic Superman, and he wasn't having any of my mortality or hesitation. He called my family to complain again, and they threatened to come back up and yell at me again, but I told them I would save them the trip and promised to shape up. In the late fall of 2006, I returned to Arizona for a tournament, where I would show them all that I was still the same old Henry, convince them that nothing had changed, that I was still the great wrestler I had always been. That I could be that great wrestler, even without that Terry Brand–ordered 1,000 percent.

Except that I wasn't. I got beaten in the first round by some dude I should have pinned, who I could've pinned with no problem a few months earlier. But it wasn't the same me. I didn't have my stamina anymore. I didn't have my strength to depend on anymore. My mind couldn't focus anymore, pushing me until my body was broken. It was humiliating. All this work for nothing.

My family sat in the stands and shook their heads. I blew them off to stagger into Clarissa's arms for comfort. Together we left Arizona and returned to Colorado Springs, where I discovered I wasn't the only one who had been slacking off. It turns out, enjoying the life as my pseudo-wife, Clarissa had also been missing practice, and had been thrown out of the wrestling room for a week.

"You don't have to be back for an entire week?" I asked her that night in her apartment.

She nodded. She should have been frowning, but instead she was smiling.

"Are you thinking what I'm thinking?" I said.

And just like that, we went AWOL. Just like that, I walked away from the sport that had created me and the dream that had defined me. All the hard work I had put in and all the hopes that I had been keeping for myself.

Without telling anyone, I threw some clothes in a duffel bag, climbed into Clarissa's truck, and together we drove the ninety miles to the Denver airport to catch a flight to San Diego for a week in the sun.

Except, well, first, before we could get to the sun, there was the snow. A surprise snowstorm shut down the airport, and we ended up spending the night on the floor of the airport terminal, two fugitives on the run, and it was kind of weird. By the time we landed in San Diego, it was totally weird. And I felt totally awful.

Our first stop in California was at the shack of a friend who lived near the beach. It was as cramped as a closet, and had no electricity, and my freaking cell phone was ringing off the hook. But I had made a commitment to Clarissa for a fun week away. I had made a commitment to myself to assert my independence. So I never answered that phone. And, dammit, I was not going home.

While the week was torture on my conscience, it was even worse on my liver. We went surfing, slide boarding, shopping, bowling, and drank. And drank. And drank.

I drank to forget the pain of the wrestling. I drank to forget the angst that surrounded my love for Clarissa. I drank because it was easy and, screw it, for once, I was going to do something easy and I wanted to do what other college-age kids—my peers—were doing. Going out and partying. Meeting new people. Forgetting about their responsibilities for a while.

It was during this trip that I realized some of the big differences in my life and Clarissa's life. We were together in spirit, but far apart in perspective and life experience.

You know how my San Diego friend lived in a shack with no electricity? We then drove up to Los Angeles to stay with one of her friends in a huge house with Louis Vuitton comforters. It sounds crazy that I would remember that kind of detail, but it has stuck with me even to this day. I was a street kid, and she was a privileged kid, and, for me, it was a difficult obstacle to overcome. Despite the fact that we were both wrestlers, that we had that in common, and were both far from home, there was too much difference between our lives and who we were and how we had grown up.

How could she understand my life spent fighting everyone over plastic McDonald's wrappers when she took her meals from a silver spoon? How could she understand my fear of failure when she could never really fail? There would always be somebody there to pick her up, rub her shoulders, give her a job, set her up back on her feet. If I failed, there was nothing waiting for me, especially not a job. There was nothing.

If she can no longer wrestle, she just goes back to the paradise of Hawaii, where she's from originally. If I can no longer wrestle, I go back to the barrio.

I started to think about my brother Alonzo and his speech about the safety net. And I started to wonder, What the hell was I doing so far from wrestling practice? That was my center, that was where I needed to be. That was what had saved me before.

After the week ended, we jumped back on a plane and hustled home. I couldn't wait to get back to that sweaty, stinky, soul-redeeming wrestling room. I couldn't wait to run up to Terry Brands and apologize for disappearing and throw myself back on the mat with renewed energy to show him just how sorry I could really be.

I went home with Clarissa, grabbed my wrestling stuff, drove back to the training center. As soon as I got there, I marched right into the wrestling room at the start of my first practice in a week, took my place among the other wrestlers, and smiled my best smile at Terry and . . .

"What do you think you're doing?" he shouted.

"Hey, Coach, I'm—"

"No, you're not," he shouted. "Get the hell out of my room!"

"But, I—"

"No, no, no," he shouted. "Get the hell out of my room!"

His room? It was my room. It was our room. I lived here. What was happening?

"Please, I—"

"I'll say it for the last time," he shouted again. "Get the hell out of my room!"

And with that, it all disappeared in a moment: my spot on the team, my dream of the Olympics, the most important place in my life.

I walked out of the room, slowed down just before I left, turned around to see if I could have one more chance, and . . .

"Get out!" he shouted.

In the span of a week, I had frittered away the hopes of a lifetime.

Although only twenty-two months away, the Olympics were once again little more than a junkyard dream.

★SEVEN★

I have slept on wooden floors, on dirty bathroom tiles, on mattresses stained an unimaginable color, next to armpits emitting an unimaginable smell. I've slept in the depths of the human condition and up on the heights of an apartment rooftop. Since leaving home, there is really only one way I haven't slept.

I haven't slept in the dark.

I can't sleep in the dark. It's physically impossible for me. My mind races and my hearts thumps and I just can't relax while alone in the blackness.

I need some sort of light, whether it comes through an open curtain or a cracked door or, okay, hell, I'll admit, even a baby night-light. Fine, go ahead, laugh all you want. I can hear the joke now, one of the toughest guys in the world and he's afraid of the dark, right?

Not exactly. I'm not afraid of the dark. I'm afraid of the solitude of the dark. I'm afraid of the quiet of the dark. I'm not used to sleeping alone, remember? Some of those first nights at the Olympic Training Center when I slept with Angel to avoid being alone in my own room? I'm also not used to sleeping in quiet, especially the kind of quiet that is never interrupted by a crazed Spanish scream or long looping siren.

When I was growing up, sleep was always the best, safest time of my day. I was surrounded by family in a nest of blankets. I was protected by my siblings' bodies, surrounded by the murmurs of their whispered conversations. They were not only my bedmates, they were my shield against the world.

Once I moved out, I missed that. Hugging a cold pillow miles away in another state is not the same as draping your arm around a warm shoulder of a brother or sister. Now, while the hardest parts of my life have become easier, the easiest part of my life has become hardest. Even though nobody else is with me, I need to know that someone else is out there. Even if that someone else is just a flickering hall light.

The first person to notice this was Mr. Hurtado, my assistant high school wrestling coach and resident mentor. I would usually hang around his house long enough to be invited to spend the night, and then I would go to bed before everyone else and sneak back to Mr. and Mrs. Hurtado's bed, which was soft and comfy and felt like it was being used even when it wasn't. Mr. Hurtado would eventually come back, find me there, and throw me out, putting me in a separate room or out on the couch, and every night, I remember he would laugh.

"Can you leave a light on for me?" I would ask.

"Big tough guy can't sleep in the dark?" he would say with a chuckle.

But he would always find a distant light and switch it on. And he would never say a word about it to anyone else. And I'll never forget him for that.

So, as you can guess now, I hated being alone. This meant that my banishment from the U.S. Wrestling team in the fall of 2006 was perhaps the worst time of my life. In a moment of youthful foolishness—well, okay, I was always a young fool— I had gone AWOL with my girlfriend, spending a week in southern California and missing practice back at the Olympic Training Center. I was supposed to be back in Colorado Springs with Terry Brands, working my butt off. I knew when I returned that I would get in trouble. But I had no idea just how much trouble.

I thought I might be thrown out of one practice and yelled at. But on my return, after my initial protests to stay in the wrestling room were answered with Terry screaming for me to leave, the ground rules were set. It was October 30, and Terry already had a date in his mind.

"November thirtieth," he told me. "Stay away from my room for the next month. Think about what you want to do. Think about who you want to be. Come back November thirtieth and tell me whether you want to wrestle here or not. One month."

One month? I could not survive one month out of the wrestling room. Absolutely not.

"You're going to be great, and you know it," he said. "You can go anywhere in the world and win. You can go join the Russian team and win. You can go to Turkey and win. And I don't care, go. But if you are going to stay here, you are going to do it my way, with my rules."

He stared me in the eye, and then ushered me out the door.

"I'll see you on November thirtieth," he said. "If you're in, you're in. If you're out, you're out."

One month? I cried to Clarissa. I complained to my mom and, finally, I begged USA Wrestling officials, speaking to them in the most adult terms I could muster.

"You brought me here as a kid; you knew what you were getting," I reminded them. "I did something dumb, but I was acting like a kid. And this kid cannot make it for a month outside the wrestling room."

The officials heard me. They approached Terry. They asked him to allow me back in the room. Now Terry was really mad. I had tried to get back into the room by going around him and trying to force his hand. He put his entire job on the line to keep me out of that room and make a point, teach me a lesson.

"Why did you hire me?" he asked the officials. "You knew my rules. You knew my methods. I am not going to be accountable for this kid not winning a gold medal if I can't do it my way."

I hated Terry for that speech. But I also loved Terry for that speech.

The officials backed him, as they should have. I stayed out of the wrestling room for a full month, which is what I deserved. It was really hard to be away from that place for a whole month, though. Imagine being told that the one sane constant in your life, that one activity that brings control, order, and a source of pride into your existence is taken away. Taken away because of some boneheaded vacation, one dumb, spur-of-the-moment decision to fly to California.

When I was allowed back into the wrestling room and came

back, I was still mad, and I still didn't totally understand, but at least I had cooled off enough to tell Terry what he wanted to hear.

"I will do anything you tell me," I told him, desperate to once again feel the mat against my body and somebody's shoulder pushing against my elbow in competition.

And I would. But I still wasn't ready to completely listen. I worked hard, but I didn't work smart. I was nineteen going on twenty-nine, perhaps the understandable product of a system where I basically skipped the two high school years that were invented to remind all of us we are still kids, and to let us all figure out who we're going to be as adults. Most others my age realized they still had a lot to learn. I thought I knew it all. I was an adult in experience and in what people expected of me, in my responsibilities, but a child in maturity.

I was back on decent terms with Terry, but still stuck sometimes in apathy and occasionally even despair. This was too hard. This was taking too long. The trip to southern California hadn't been a long enough break for me to let off steam. Where was the end? How could I last long enough to win my gold?

Every time my mother came to Colorado Springs, where she eventually moved, I would hug her and kiss her and cling to her. She would rub my back and whisper that everything would be okay, but it was obvious that I needed more than words, and I needed more than a mother's touch. The more I worked myself up into this angst, the more I needed someone bigger than me to kick my butt and pull me out of it. The more I needed a male role model who understood me, who unconditionally loved me, who was a part of me.

For the first time in my life, I needed my father.

Ah, yes, the missing Jorge Cejudo. Or, if you prefer, the missing Favian Roca. Or Javier Zaragosa. Or Emiliano Zaragosa. For someone who had no real identity, and no real presence in my life, my father sure had plenty of names. It was actually fitting that he had all these aliases, because he was constantly on the lam from his family as well as the authorities.

You'll remember, the last time I saw him, I was five years old, we were at the circus, and the police basically broke down the door of the big top to arrest him. When he was finally released from jail, you'll remember that my mother was so afraid he would attempt to harm us, she hurriedly moved us to New Mexico, thus beginning our life as nomads. Yeah, my father was never there when we needed him, and frighteningly there when we wanted no part of him.

After we fled from him, even though his name was never really spoken in our household, I would still think about him occasionally, especially during those times when a boy just needs a dad.

Once in Arizona, I was picked up by the cops for stealing a candy bar with a buddy. I was only about eight years old at the time, so the cop took pity on me and drove me to my house, where my mom delivered unto me an unholy beating that was far worse than jail. With each whack on my butt from her long stick, I would yell at my mother but be thinking about my father.

My dad would have understood what it was like to be hungry and alone on deserted aisle 5. My dad would have understood my impulse for survival. My dad would have also understood my need to be reckless, to take chances, to make my mark myself by being different, even if it only meant sticking a stupid candy bar in my pocket and trying to sneak out with it.

"Mommy!" my voice shrieked then.

"Daddy," my heart cried.

Then there was the time a few years later when Angel and I were the stars of our neighborhood's youth soccer team, leading us to the championship game against some suburban white kids with shiny minivans and portable lawn chairs and Keebler's packaged snacks. We were much better athletes than those kids. But, as it turned out, we weren't nearly as smart about the sport, about strategy and working together as a team, and so they whacked us 9–2, a beating so bad that near the end of the game, Angel and I were fighting. Not with the other team, but with each other, screaming at each other and then punching each other, right there on the field while the ball rolled past us and into our own goal. We were too distracted with the trouble we were causing each other to even notice.

Yeah, my mother beat us good that time too. And, yeah, once again, I wished my dad had been there. He would have known what to say to stop us before we started. Our anger came from his anger, so he would have understood the flash in Angel's eyes or the tone in my voice as I challenged him. He would have sensed us starting to fight, and would have stopped the game to pull us out before the embarrassing incident happened and the fists started to fly.

I could have used my dad in some big incidents as well as the little ones, like the decision to allow me to go to Colorado Springs. I later learned that my mother and sisters didn't sleep for several nights before agreeing to let me go. They worried that I would be molested. They worried that I would get put out on the street if I didn't do well. They thought, as they often thought when I left home for any length of time, that I would be kidnapped. That would have been a brilliant criminal maneuver, kidnapping a kid with no money, no assets, and no influence. What would be the ransom? My mother's tamales? Our blankets? A crazy idea, but they couldn't get it out of their heads.

I could have used my dad in that transitional time. While my mother trusted Tracy, she would have listened more to a man who was her husband. He would have quieted their fears. He would have understood the opportunity. Heck, he would have probably driven me there.

So, yeah, I missed him. And it turns out I wasn't the only one. When I was twelve, my older sister Gloria actually quit her job to fly to Mexico City to see him. He had moved there shortly after we had left California, and, because of all his legal troubles in the United States, he never moved back.

Gloria had to sneak away for the trip, because my mother would have never approved. Gloria knew where he was staying because she had quietly kept in touch with our aunts and uncles. Unfortunately, she had no idea *what* he was. And what she found sickened her.

My father had become one of the doctors at an alcohol rehabilitation center, which sounds like a great gig, but there were two problems. He wasn't a doctor. And he was still an alcoholic himself. My sister remembers meeting him there one morning and hugging him and smelling liquor on his breath. He was still a con man. He was still hurting people. And he was still not in any position to help us. Gloria gave him our phone number anyway, and came home with the biggest smile she could muster.

"Who knows?" she said, running her hands through my hair like a mother comforting a baby. "Maybe Daddy will call you."

Sure enough, about a week later he called the home phone late one night, and having just arrived from wrestling practice, I was the one who picked it up.

"Hello?" I said cautiously, as I always did when answering a phone because it was usually a bill collector.

"Henry? Is that you?" said a heavily accented voice.

"Um, yes?" I said, thinking it was some strange wrestling coach whose name I'd forgotten.

"Henry, it's your father," said the voice.

"Daddy!" I screamed excitedly, this time for real, and one of those conversations you remember for your entire life began. One of those conversations you play over and over in your head later in life.

He asked if I was staying tough. He asked if I was being the man of the house and helping out. I lowered my voice and answered the questions with all the bravado that a twelve-year-old could muster. Yes, I was tough. Yes, indeed, I was the man around here.

And then he asked me for money.

I don't remember the exact words, but I'll never forget the exact feeling. He had robbed us of everything from our Christmas presents to our childhood, and now he was also wanting our money?

I didn't know what to say. At the time, between the two of us, Angel and I had exactly one pair of used wrestling shoes and one pair of used tennis shoes. One day he would wear the wrestling shoes and I would wear the tennis shoes, and then the next day we would switch. At night, at home, lying next to each other with those shoes crumpled up in the corner, we would each know that our lives would be so much easier if only we had a father, so at least maybe we could have our own pair of shoes. Surely he would have bought us some new ones so we wouldn't have to share.

And now that man was asking me for money?

I hurriedly said, "Goodbye, Daddy," and handed the phone to Gloria. I wasn't as mad as I was stunned. I couldn't even talk. Gloria soon hung up the phone, in the same condition. I wish I had been older. I wish I had been more patient, smarter, more understanding, and kept him on the phone talking about something else. I wish I could've told him about my wrestling or about how the other Cejudo kids were doing.

I wish I had known then that I would never speak to my father again.

As time passed, and my success became great, I tried to forget about that phone call and focused only on the father of my dreams. How I wished he could have seen me win just one of my four state championships. It was no coincidence that the kids I beat the worst in those tournaments were the kids who showed up with their dads. Seeing a father send his son out to the mat with an encouraging pat on the back enraged me. How weak that the kid couldn't take care of himself! How sad and pathetic that I was so jealous!

Everyone has always asked me why I would hang out after the meets and keep working out, keep wrestling kids who wanted to challenge me. One of the reasons was that I couldn't bear to leave the building next to kids who were walking out with their fathers' arms around their shoulders. I might have had the gold, but they had the dads, making them much, much richer.

I wished my father could have seen me become the first high school wrestler to win the senior nationals in 2006, a tournament featuring all the best wrestlers in the United States, many of them in their late twenties. Can you imagine? I wish I had looked up into the stands and seen him there. When I won the national title again in the spring of 2007, I couldn't take it anymore. My heart hurt worse than my elbows or back after the match. I had officially become a tough guy, but I wanted my father to see his toughness in me. I wanted him to see the determination he gave me. I wanted to both brag about myself, and compliment him on creating such a warrior.

I also wondered, What the hell was he like? Did he look like me? Did he have my pug nose? Did he have my prickly sense of humor? Did he work hard like me? Did he crave hugs like me? Was he afraid to sleep in the dark like me? Who was this man? This stranger?

I was going to be an official twenty-one-year-old adult in less than a year, and it was time to satisfy the single toughest hunger of my childhood. I was done wishing my dad could see me. Instead, I became determined to go to Mexico City to see him.

I bought the plane ticket with money from my national winners' check, and promptly announced to my family that I was going to see Daddy.

You should have seen the looks on their faces. It was like they had just seen a ghost. As it turns out, they were more fearful that I was going only to see a ghost when I got there.

"No, you can't go," said Gloria quickly, almost too quickly

"Why not?" I demanded.

"Because, um, er, we were planning a big trip to see him together in a couple of months!" she said.

"How come I didn't know about these plans?" I said.

"You know now!" she said.

At this point, my brother Alonzo chipped in.

"Dude, this is going to be a family thing. Don't let down the family," he said.

"Why am I just hearing about this now?" I said.

Later I learned they had discovered that my father was living on the streets in Mexico, shooting heroin in alleys, beating up his girlfriend—his only real possession a transistor radio.

Down deep, they thought that if I saw him in this condition, it would mess me up so badly that I would not recover from the shock and it would ruin my chances at the Olympics. Worse yet, they thought my father might kidnap me and kill me if the family didn't give him all of our worldly possessions. For once, when it came to the bizarre kidnapping scenario, I guess it made sense.

But they admitted none of this to me at the time. To me, they said it was all about . . . bonding?

"C'mon, Henry, it will be a great family trip. We'll bond with each other and with Daddy; just wait a few months," said Gloria.

"How many months?" I said.

"We'll go in July. I've—I've actually already bought the tickets," she said.

"Oh, so now you've bought the tickets?" I said.

The entire thing sounded fishy to me. But my family had never lied to me. My family has never played tricks on me. I trusted them more than anyone else in the world besides Tracy. If they thought I should wait to see my father, then I would wait.

Those tickets I bought for Mexico City? I turned them into a Terry Brands–sanctioned trip to Cancún with Clarissa. I was convinced there would be time to return to see my father. I was young, I was unbeatable, and there was always time.

Then, of course, there wasn't.

In May of 2007, shortly after I returned to Colorado Springs from Cancún, I received a phone call from my mother. Officials summoned me out of wrestling practice to take the call, so I knew it had to be serious. When I picked up the phone, she was speaking in Spanish, so I knew right away that it was real serious.

"Tu padre esta muerto," she said.

Your father is dead.

He was forty-four years old and had succumbed to an alcohol-related illness.

"Tu padre esta muerto," she repeated.

Your father is dead.

He was just starting to come to life for me as I thought we were planning this trip to see him, yet now my father was dead? I could have still been in Mexico hugging him and loving him, yet my family talked me out of it, and now my father was dead? I had spoken to him once in fifteen years, and now my father was dead?

I sat down outside the training center wrestling room and softly cried. Then I loudly screamed.

"Screw them, screw them, screw my family!" I shouted. "How could they do this to me? How could they keep me from my father!"

The phone rang again. It was my brother Alonzo. I think he knew what I was feeling. I know for sure that he heard me sobbing, and he immediately tried to stop it.

"Dude, do not cry for that piece of crap. All he did was hurt us!" he shouted. "No tears for him! No tears! He was an awful man who didn't care about us!"

"Screw you!" I shouted back to him. "Screw all of you!"

I put down the phone again, cried some more, and screamed some more.

"I don't care what he did!" I shouted to nobody. "He was my father! I have lost my father!"

I walked inside the wrestling room and proceeded to have the best, and worst, practice of my life. For two hours I was everywhere, throwing guys on their backs, bouncing myself off the mat, taking out my rage on a bunch of wide-eyed teammates who thought I had lost my mind.

Then, during the middle of practice, in the middle of the brawling, I started bawling. I knew then that I really had lost my mind. No matter how badly I hurt during workouts, I would never show pain or fear, and I would never cry—I was never going to be a baby. Yet here I was, a complete crying mess, and for a moment, as crazy as it sounds, I was ashamed.

I finished the practice, and immediately drove to Angel's apartment, where several members of my family were staying, including my mother. Once I got there and saw them for the first time since learning the news, I screamed at them some more. I accused them of sabotaging my relationship with the man who had created my life. I accused them of robbing me of a chance—the final chance—to hang out with a guy who I always imagined could have been my best friend. I accused them of murder in the first degree, of murdering my heritage and my home and the kinship I could have had with my father.

"Okay, fine," said Gloria finally, interrupting my rampage. "Now we'll go."

So we went, Gloria and Angel and I, the three of us flying down to Mexico City later that summer to finally, sadly, find our father and to say our goodbyes. We first stopped at some relatives' homes there, which opened my reddened, sad eyes to the fact that, as our lives were improving, my father's life had been imploding. We stayed at a cousin's hut that didn't have indoor plumbing—I had to walk down a hill to use the bathroom. The trash all around was awful; the stench was unbearable. We saw the nearby shack where my father lived out his life—it was no bigger than a closet, with no windows, only a blanket on the floor. It brought back memories of Las Cruces, memories of long, long ago.

My father was not a rich man. He was not an influential man. He was not a powerful man. My father was, well, he was a bum. He had turned on his family, left them, and become a bum.

But, dammit, he was my bum, and I insisted on seeing where he was buried.

"Are you sure?" asked Gloria.

"I've never been more sure of anything in my life," I said.

So we drove through a blighted neighborhood and stopped suddenly next to an empty dirt field adjacent to a giant Dumpster.

"What are we doing?" I asked Gloria, looking around.

"This is it," she said.

This was a graveyard? People were buried here? My father was buried here? I stepped outside the car and walked across the dirt to discover little cinder blocks set up on tiny plots. There were no headstones with names and dates engraved on them. There were no marble statues or mausoleums with angels. There weren't even any flowers left to commemorate the dead there.

But this was a graveyard, my father's graveyard. This was where he would spend eternity. This was where I had to face my memory of him and finally get on with my life.

A relative pointed to the bit of dirt that covered Dad, and I immediately dropped to my knees where he pointed. My dad was six feet away. After fifteen years and thousands of miles, my daddy was now just six feet beneath me.

My sister said I turned white. She said I acted as if something had possessed me, and she was right. I think in that moment, my father possessed me. Suddenly, the man who created me was right at my fingertips, and I needed to feel him, needed to feel that he had been real.

I scooped up the dirt from the area around his grave and began running it through my fingers. This was part of him. This was as close as I would ever get to him now. I wanted him near me. I wanted him with me. As I washed the dirt over my hands, I started crying, and soon the soil was mixing with the tears, streaks of brown mud in my palms.

"What are you doing!?" shouted Gloria.

"I'm hugging Daddy!" I sobbed. "I'm finally hugging Daddy!"

As I wept, I continued to immerse myself in what I imagined were his remains. I then fell face-first into the soil and just lay there, breathing in the last memories of a man I never knew. I was in my own world of grief, when all of a sudden I heard my sister shouting.

"Get up!" shouted Gloria. "Get the hell up!"

"I'm touching him!" I cried. "I'm finally touching him!"

"Get the hell up and listen to me!" shouted Gloria. "Listen to me!"

With that, she began listing every awful thing that my father had done to my family—the stolen presents, the stolen money, the death threats, the abandonment, the drugs, the general lawlessness.

"I know you loved him, Henry, but he was a piece of crap!" she shouted down at my dirt-stained body as I lay there. "Look where he's buried! By a Dumpster! You reap what you sow, Henry!"

"But he's my father and I never—"

"Listen to me! Wipe that dirt off your hands and bury him! Bury that son of a bitch! Bury him forever. Get up out of here and get on with your life!"

"But I loved him and I never—"

"God cut his life short so you wouldn't have to see him in such bad shape, Henry! God wants you to move on. So move on!"

Finally she had said something that hit me, that got through to me in my fog of grief. I could finally hear her and understand her message loud and clear.

And here's what I came to understand. God cut my father's life short so I could carry on the burden that he couldn't bear, take it on my own shoulders. God took my father's life so I could live and fulfill the lessons he would never teach me and never have the chance to teach me. God took him away before I could get to him so I would spend the rest of my life reaching out for him and in doing so, always push myself farther and harder to prove myself.

My father may have been a bum, but every bit of strength and courage he had, I had within me now. My father may have abandoned me physically, but I felt that he was forever in me, in my heart and mind. And now that he was gone so young, it was my job to show the world his potential, to live the sort of life that fate and his troubles did not allow him to live, to be a better him, in his image, forever and ever amen.

I would eventually shower and the mud from his grave would wash off of me and down the drain, but I knew that in some way, this dirt would stay with me always. It would cake my conscience, and it would coat my heart. It would remind me of the frailty of the human condition, of the fine line between greatness and despair, of how I could redeem my father not simply through survival, but triumph.

"I think I get it," I told Gloria as I slowly stood up, the dirt of my father's grave falling off my jeans and T-shirt, pooling around my tennis shoes.

I brushed myself off. I patted down the dirt on the small plot. I stared down, toward six feet under, knowing I would never look in this direction again.

"Bury the bastard," my sister whispered to me. "Bury the bastard, and go win that gold medal."

The burial part took longer than I thought. It damn near took another year before I could mentally put my father into his grave. While in some ways my father's death had freed to me to chase my wildest dreams, the fact that I never said goodbye in person also weighed on my mind. I was now wrestling not only for one, but two—in memory of my father—and I initially crumbled under the added weight.

I felt that extra weight at first a few months later at the world championships in September of 2007, in the distant country of Azerbaijan, in central Asia. Here I was, the reigning 121-pound wrestling champion in the greatest country in the world, facing the greatest wrestlers in the world, all the way around the world from home, and what happened? I didn't score a point. I was beaten in my first match, and didn't score a one single freaking point. I spent two days traveling halfway around the world and I was on the mat for all of about four minutes, and lost each of the first two rounds in the best-of-three format, and that was that. I didn't score a damn point.

How embarrassing. How awful. The next morning, instead of getting up and running like I always did, I stayed in bed and wept. I had lost my father, and now I felt like I had lost my wrestling life, and it only got worse.

I returned home to the United States and began to get busy losing to everyone in sight. I lost in the first round of dual meets to guys I had never heard of. I'm serious. I stopped listening to Terry, who was working with me to adjust my aggressive style. I stopped listening to my family, who kept telling me to work harder and move on from my dad's death. I felt like there had been another death in the family. That death was me and my focus and passion.

Looking back, maybe I was finally burned out, all the years working toward this goal, all the pressures of fulfilling this impossible dream finally crushing me in the final run-up to the Olympics. Or maybe I just needed to get my ass handed to me before I could once again appreciate winning. Or maybe I just sucked. Well, for sure, I sucked, and I continued losing all over the world, sometimes being pinned a minute into the match. It was less than a year before the Olympics, and it was a wonder they still kept me on the national team. It was less than a year before my ultimate goal, and right now, it would be a miracle if I even made the Olympic team, much less medaled.

I don't think the thirty-first-best 121-pound wrestler in the world had ever finished in the top three in the Olympics less than a year later. Hell, I would be lucky if they didn't throw me out of Colorado Springs entirely and send me packing back to Arizona.

In late January of 2008, I traveled to Russia long enough to be caught quickly in a half-nelson and pinned by another inferior opponent, and it was time to leave again. I was fed up with all this losing.

"I need a week off," I told Terry. "I'm doing my best, but it's just not there. I need a week off. Please."

Amazingly, he gave it to me. He told me to disappear for a week and come back ready to try again. I realized that Terry understood I was trying to do something no American freestyle wrestler had ever done—go from high school to the Olympics to the medal podium. Terry understood how hard this was for me to step back and reevaluate how I was going to achieve my dream, and how difficult my situation off the mat, outside of the wrestling room, was at that time.

From the moment Terry arrived at the training center in 2005, I thought I was cursed to have him as a coach. After nearly three years, though, I finally realized I was blessed.

Terry understood. But that doesn't mean I was able to respond. I kept losing, and finally it hit bottom in February of 2008 in a dual meet in Albuquerque, New Mexico. I had made my triumphant return there as a hometown boy who made good, if you ignore the fact that I wasn't exactly born there and that I lived there only long enough to become a Mexican gang's mascot. It seemed my entire old neighborhood from Las Cruces had shown up to cheer me on and watch me wrestle—minus the

AutoZone clerks and Chinese restaurant waiters—and everyone was going crazy for me.

And I gave them nothing. Zilch. Nada. Nothing. I lost two
dual matches to a Belarus wrestler who I should have pounded;
neither match was close. The fans who had come to see me were
stunned, the cheers evaporated, the balloons disappeared. It was
like I had popped the sweet bubble of my youthful potential and
promise and left everyone dripping and sticky and mad with my
broken dreams.

I grabbed my stuff and started heading back to the hotel
when I was stopped by two young brown-faced kids. Their cheeks
were dirty, their tennis shoes were scuffed, but their little bodies were buffed, popping out of little wrestling shirts. These
weren't just two tiny strangers. These two kids were once me.

I smiled and bent down to sign their autographs when I realized they had no paper or pen. They only had these sad stares as
they looked up at me.

"What happened?" they said. "What happened to you?"

I hustled back to the hotel, climbed on the treadmill, turned
it to full-blast speed, and began crying. Running and crying, the
tears of sadness at my father's death now becoming the tears of
anger at the poor way I was handling the situation. I was once
those kids, and I was about two more losses away from becoming those kids again. I once had nothing, and I was just about
one half-nelson away from having nothing again.

Bullshit. This wasn't going to happen to me. That wasn't
me. I was Henry Cejudo, the kid who has beaten the crap out
of other kids in apartment courtyards and national wrestling
meets alike, the kid who has embraced fear and danced on ad-
versity. I was Henry Cejudo, tough son of Jorge Cejudo, proud

son of Nelly Rico, blessed son of the United States of America. Many people in my country had sacrificed themselves for me, or sacrificed themselves to me, and now it was time to pay them back and show them that it was all worth it.

My father, finally, was buried. My mission, finally, was clear. I wasn't just going to fight for myself and my past and my father. I was going to fight for my country. For all the kids like me, and all the kids who weren't like me. I was going to fight for everyone who had once believed in me.

The next morning, I phoned up Terry Brands.

"Terry, if you will be my general, I will be your soldier," I told him.

"Let's get your ass back to work," he said.

From there, the final six months to the Olympics were all a blur. Working eight hours a day with Terry, I learned to channel my aggressiveness, to use my brains in conjunction with my passion, to fight not only harder, but smarter. To fight with heart, but also with my head.

I won the Pan American championships in February of 2008, beating a world bronze medalist from Cuba, Andy Gonzalez, which was huge because by me winning a continental title, it qualified the United States for the Olympics at 121 pounds. Then I lost the national finals in April of 2008 to a veteran named Matt Azevedo. He actually pinned me, but I was okay. I knew exactly what had happened, why it had happened, and where I had gone wrong. It was a mistake of overaggression that I would not make again, and I learned from the loss and moved on to the Olympic Trials on the great end of the draw.

What happened was that Azevedo and 2004 Olympic silver medalist Stephen Abas (my other big competitor) were in the same side of the bracket. I was on the other side of bracket. I had gotten lucky—the luck of the draw, literally. So one of them would be eliminated before the winner of that bracket wrestled me. I still had to beat a guy who would later qualify for the world team, a guy who grew up down the road from where I grew up, a Phoenix guy named Danny Felix, but once I did that, I was in the Olympic Trials finals. On the other side of the bracket, the one who got eliminated ended up being Azevedo, putting me in the finals against Abas, and when I heard that, the memories came rushing back.

Remember when I was younger and saw him at a meet and my mentor, Tracy Greiff, had urged me to go over and talk to him? Remember how I told Tracy that I didn't want to get friendly with someone I would have to beat one day, didn't want to get emotionally involved? So I purposefully ignored him?

Well, here he was, standing in front of me, and I could ignore him no more. It was a best-of-three freestyle event. Not best-of-three rounds, like the Olympics, but best-of-three matches, which means as many as nine rounds, all in the same day. So, yeah, it's a crazy amount of wrestling, basically an entire day of wrestling squeezed into half of that time, a test not only of expertise and skill, but of endurance. We split the first two matches, and we were climbing all over each other for twelve total minutes, and we were both exhausted.

Abas saw me catch my breath a moment, and quickly made a move that gave him a 1–0 lead after the first round of the final match. I knew he thought I was a weak, young, inexperienced kid. I knew he thought I would crumble under his skill and under the pressure. But I knew he had no idea that being down 1–0 with possibly only two minutes remaining to achieve your dream was the sort of deficit I had been faced with forever.

Trailing in the last minutes with the match on the line? I was right at home. Coming back from behind, coming up from the depths. And soon I was going to China, as I dominated him for each of the final two rounds, winning each 3–0 to win the whole match and qualify for the Olympics.

I had done it! I wearily raised my hands above my head, and I hoarsely screamed to my family who were watching me. I weakly hugged Tracy. I was going to the Olympics. I knew it now. But the road there had been tough enough to drain much of the instant joy from me, and it was a road that, perhaps fittingly, would not end until the moment I climbed on that plane to China.

You see, I still had to deal with the other love of my life—Clarissa Chun. I had handled wrestling and my resurrection on the mat, and now I had to handle the passion of the other part of my life. By then, our relationship seemed like destiny when you realize that I advanced to the Olympics only by beating her former boyfriend, Abas, while at the same time, she was advancing to the Olympics by beating my former partner, Patricia Miranda.

By then we could have been a storybook couple . . . if we had not already endured a gossip-magazine breakup.

The actual split occurred about nine months earlier, just before Thanksgiving of 2007. I was worried that Clarissa's presence in my life was distracting me from my goals in wrestling, and I'm sure she was also worried that my presence was only, like, ruining her life.

I certainly ruined one of her cars, sliding it into a tree the previous winter, driving it while she was home in Hawaii, an event typical of my immature attitude toward the relationship and her stuff. I didn't know how to use the four-wheel drive, and I thought it automatically kicked in, so as I drove it, the truck had no traction and smashed into a tree trunk, breaking the rearview mirror and seriously damaging the driver's-side door.

When I called her in Hawaii and confessed to her about it, I promised to fix it. But I never did. I didn't have the money, and I drove around with what I called "Mexican insurance." Which means, of course, that I had no insurance. For a year, until Clarissa finally fixed it herself, I'm sure that battered truck symbolized the fact that I was a much younger, completely irresponsible dude who needed to grow up. I am sorry for that. And I am sorry for the way that I finally extricated myself from this mismatched situation.

Basically, during that winter of 2007, I hid. I broke up with her, and then I ran straight over to Angel's apartment and hid out, camped out in his bedroom while she rightfully came after me for an explanation. She never got any farther than my mother, who had never wanted us together in the first place. My mother met her at the front door while holding a cane that she uses for support and strength. In her other hand, she had an iron, and she was prepared to wield them both.

"It's over," my mother told Clarissa in English.

Then, later, my mother and Angel actually drove to Clarissa's apartment and removed my stuff for me, what little stuff I had there. I am sad to say that I was not man enough to do it myself. I could break down some of the strongest men in the world and flip them on their backs, but I didn't even have the guts to break up with my girlfriend face-to-face.

It wasn't a surprise to her. It didn't really even hurt her, I hope. I know she was ready to get rid of me and my selfish, immature ways. She deserved someone older, smarter, more mature, and she knew it.

So the breakup was amicable, even fruitful, as both of us shed the baggage of the relationship to soar, pure and free, to Beijing. We still talked; we still shared, and sometimes we still even hung out. We were both chasing our dream together, and it was a similar dream, and we appreciated that.

Well, until this one last complication. Story of my life, huh? There is always one last complication to make what could be a sane situation something nuts.

It was only three days before we left for China. I went to visit Clarissa for one last pep talk. We were both really stressed out, trying to get things and ourselves ready for the trip, and we probably should have avoided each other—avoided everyone— because we were both racked with anxiety over the upcoming trip.

But that's not me, is it? Oh, no, I can never just sit back and do the easy, sensible thing, can I?

So that night, I arrived at her apartment before she got there. I phoned her, and she said she was on her way, so I waited out front, but it took her another thirty minutes, and I called her again and yelled at her for being late.

By the time she arrived, she was furious.

"I don't appreciate you yelling at me for being late," she said.

"All the times in my life you've kept me waiting, you had no right to get mad."

She was right. But being my immature self and being already worked up, this just made me madder. So I started picking on her, joking about her appearance, inventing flaws in a woman who I already knew was absolutely flawless. She went to the bedroom to change clothes, and I shouted insults about her body to her from the kitchen, and it was horrible. I can't believe how horrible I was then.

You simply don't do this to Olympic athletes. You just don't do this. Olympians are this country's finest physical specimens, and you would think they would be the most physically secure people on earth. But what drives them to reach this beauty is a dark insecurity that they will never be perfect enough. And if the perfection is questioned by another Olympian, well, it can be crushing.

I knew this. But I was mad at Clarissa and I knew these barbs would hurt her, and if right about now you realize there are times I can be a complete jerk, well, I agree. The competitiveness that turns me into a winner on the mat is also the competitiveness that can turn me into an asshole sometimes in real life if I don't channel it the right way.

I had lost Clarissa months earlier, and I had just lost the argument about her being late. I suddenly felt like a high school kid trying to measure up to a twenty-something supermodel. For the first time since meeting Clarissa, I felt way out of my league. So, of course, I had to foolishly swing for the fences.

Not only did I find fault in her physique, but I also committed another high crime against a fellow Olympian. I ate her favorite fruit—mangoes. To a high-level athlete who thrives on fruits and vegetables and is very protective of her stock, that was a real crime. She had a bag of mangoes on the corner of her kitchen counter, and while she was in the bedroom changing clothes, in between my verbal rips, I took a bunch of big bites out of the mangoes, leaving them unrecognizable and inedible.

When she came out of the bedroom and saw the mango remnants, she lost it.

"You cockroach!" she screamed at me.

Then I lost it. I didn't let anybody call me a cockroach, even when I actually was acting like a cockroach. I grew up with cockroaches. I ate dinner around cockroaches as a kid. I slept with cockroaches. They are the lowest of the lowest of creatures. They are bottom-dwellers that I had spent my life trying to escape, and now my former girlfriend, someone I looked up to and trusted and admired, was calling me one?

To her, a native Hawaiian, it was a common insult along the lines of "idiot" or "fool."

To me, it was a stab directly into my bruised heart.

"Cockroach!" she screamed again, and that was it, I had heard enough.

"I'm out of here!" I shouted, turning my back and walking down the apartment stairs.

Whomp! Ungh! I suddenly felt a familiar weight on my back. I had felt this weight many times on a wrestling mat. But I never felt this weight trembling with this much anger.

It was Clarissa. She had followed me down the stairs and jumped on my back to either keep me from leaving or hurt me for staying. I wasn't sure which at that point.

And I didn't have time to ask. Her arms closed around my neck as she held me tighter. I felt my knees knocking and my breath quickening, so I turned and tossed her off me and grabbed her by the neck to make her stop and settle her down and pull her away from me.

Yeah, I grabbed her. I am ashamed to have done it. I am embarrassed to admit it. I know I was acting in self-defense, to stop her and calm her down, but in hindsight, that is no defense. Especially not a guy against a girl, or between two people who loved each other, no matter how much time we had spent grappling on a mat.

I grabbed her, and there was no excuse. I grabbed her, and in that moment I felt like the kind of thug that I had spent my life trying to avoid. In that moment I was no better than the worst of my past. I was no better than the worst of my father. Hell, in that moment I became my father.

She had jumped me, but she was a woman. She naturally wasn't as strong, and I had no right to push her back with my strength. I should have stood there and taken it. She had clearly thought I would stand there and take it. So she was as stunned as I was when I fought back.

"What are you doing?" she screamed.

I had no idea. I quickly removed my hands and started to apologize but, of course, it was too late. She turned and ran into her room screaming that she was calling the police, and I made no move to stop her.

This was it. I was exhausted all of a sudden. This was the end. I felt like it was the end of everything. The naturally imbued violence that had brought me to the precipice of my Olympic dream was also going to be the exact thing that kept me from that dream, turning it toxic. You wrestle hard on the mat, maybe you make it to the Olympics. If you wrestle your girlfriend, even if she's a wrestler herself, you're in big trouble.

She came back and I immediately continued apologizing to her, truly not thinking about the police, but thinking more about the horror of my actions. Where I come from, you almost expect the police to show up one day and take you away for something so, honestly, I feared more for the loss of my humanity and for Clarissa's approval than for the presence of the police.

But after about fifteen minutes, when there was a knock on the door, okay, then I was afraid of the police. Clarissa had calmed down, her neck was unmarked, and she was fine, I had only held her for a couple of seconds, and I had sincerely apologized. But now that I heard that knock, suddenly I was thinking in a panic again.

If those cops walk in that door, my Olympic dreams are done. They walk in that door, my stay at Colorado Springs was over. They walk in that door, and suddenly, the only wrestling I'll ever do again is the kind you see on TV with oversized guys attacking each other in masks and tights. So at that moment I thought, What if they don't come through that door? What if they don't know we're here? What if Clarissa and I can both agree that I screwed up but didn't deserve to miss the Olympics? I did not deserve for her to broker a deal with me, and I did not deserve her mercy, so I did not ask. I stayed silent and hoped for her mercy. But I also did not answer the door. I literally held my breath and waited. And waited. And waited. The cops knocked again. And again. And again.

I didn't move. Amazingly, neither did Clarissa. She sat there with me, stared at that knocking door, and then glared at me with eyes I will never forget. They were eyes that said, "I am going to save your life here, but you owe the world to never do this again to anybody."

After a bit, the cops left, and soon afterward, with my shirt soaked and my legs trembling, I also left.

I will never forget, or be able to properly thank, Clarissa for the undeserved mercy she showed me that night. I can only imagine she knew how devastated I would be if I couldn't go to the Olympics, if I had come this far and been sidelined due to my own stupidity and recklessness. I felt horrible. As I drove home I thought, I will pay her back. I will pay the world back. I will be a better person, and I will go the Olympics and I will win and I will prove it to everyone.

Three days later, representing the best of the best of the United States of America, I flew to Beijing.

Feeling like a total cockroach.

★EIGHT★

Standing amid the world's greatest athletes at the opening ceremonies of the world's greatest athletic event, I was smothered with a certain undeniable, unaccountable, unbelievable something.

That something was a smell.

It was the strongest smell that I had ever experienced among human beings. It was the nastiest smell of anything that wasn't a clogged toilet in a Las Cruces crack house.

My first impression of the 2008 Olympics in Beijing was that, man oh man, it stunk.

It wasn't the air, although the air should have reeked, because it was so polluted that every daylight hour looked like dusk, the smog so great you needed night-vision goggles to see the buildings across the street.

It wasn't the people, although there were millions of them packed together in searing heat and dripping humidity, swarms on every street corner, smushed together on every sidewalk. The most people I had ever seen in one place at one time in my life— hordes of humanity.

No, on this lovely Friday night in August of 2008, this greatest of smells came from the greatest citizens of the greatest of countries as they participated in the greatest of Olympic traditions. As we marched into the Beijing Olympic stadium for the opening ceremonies, that bad smell came from me and the other Olympians from the United States of America.

It was sweat. And it was easy to explain. Billions watched on worldwide television as thousands of athletes paraded into the strangely and beautifully designed "Bird's Nest" stadium structure in their fancy uniforms and bright smiles, but few saw what happened before we marched to the center of the field.

It may be one of the most beautiful ceremonies in sport, but ask any athlete who was there, it is also one of the most poorly planned ceremonies in sports. In order to get into line for the parade, all the athletes had to arrive about five hours earlier. I knew that the countries marched inside in alphabetical order, so at that point, I popped the important question.

"Are we 'A' or 'U'?" I asked one of the officials organizing us.

"What the hell are you talking about?" he said.

"Are we 'America' or 'United States of America'?" I said.

"We are USA, which means we are nearly the last group to march, which means chill out," he said.

Six hundred or so American athletes and I did the exact opposite. Standing outside in ninety-degree heat while wearing sport coats and ties and caps, we sweated it out instead of chilled out. And so, yeah, we smelled.

Every athlete from every country waits in that line. Every athlete complains about the weariness of that wait. But nobody ever talks about the stink.

Damn, it was awful, the sweat and stench rising from the blacktop waiting area. When they finally called upon us to march into the stadium, I was soaking wet and could barely stand to even twist around and smell myself.

Another strange thing happened on the way inside the Bird's Nest. There were no water bottles allowed, yet athletes from every country were sneaking them inside their jackets or socks. But many athletes were also bringing in empty water bottles.

"What's up with the empties?" I asked one of the veteran American athletes.

"You'll see," he said with a laugh.

About six hours later, I queasily saw. As we were all standing in the middle of the field, no restroom in sight, and no way to possibly reach one amid the thousands of athletes swarming, superstars from all over the world were unzipping their pants and peeing into the bottles. I couldn't believe my eyes. It was difficult to celebrate the moment while politely averting my eyes.

It's hard to get sentimental about reciting the venerable Olympic oath, or appreciating the majesty of the Olympic flag, when dudes standing next to you are giving volunteer urine samples.

I wasn't watching it on TV back home, so I'm not entirely certain here, but I'm guessing that NBC didn't show that part.

Television also didn't show a detailed video of our team meeting, in the nearby fencing venue, then-President George W. Bush and his father, President George H. W. Bush. It was the only time in my life that I've been starstruck. I mean, the younger Bush was the main man, the guy in charge of the greatest place in the world, and, for once, I didn't know what to say. As I shook his hand, I lapsed into my Phoenix barrio accent. I had no idea that he would then lapse into his Texas twang.

"What's up, Mr. President!" I said.

"Doin' great," he said, grabbing my hand.

"Whaddya think?" I said.

"Gawd, I loooove this country," he said.

Thank you, Mr. President. I had my motto, my theme, the quote that I used throughout the Olympics to inspire myself and to explain this feeling to others. Many thought I was using it as a joke, and it was kind of funny, but after a while it really stuck with me and I couldn't get it out of my head or my heart.

"Gawd, I loooove this country," I would say to everyone.

And, God, walking into the stadium that night, despite the smell and the bladder issues, I really did love this country. Surrounded by hundreds of other athletes wearing red, white, and blue, marching strong into a stadium of wary-eyed foreigners, I have never before felt closer to the heart of America.

As we finally made our way to the end of an underground tunnel, the giant field opening up beyond us, the entire American contingent started hooting and hollering and acting like little kids.

"USA! USA! USA!" we cheered, bouncing up and down with each syllable. And you thought only the fans chanted that, huh?

When we finally started walking down the track, I smartly hung out next to the guys who got all the cheers. You know, my boys Kobe and Melo. Sure, Kobe Bryant and Carmelo Anthony wouldn't know me from a ball boy, but members of the USA basketball team were clearly the stars of the show, and I wanted to be in their posse.

Fans screamed at them, took photos of them, waved wildly at them, and after a while I started to get confused about them. I mean, they were nice guys and all, but what is the difference between them and me? Only about seven feet difference in height, maybe, but what else? Do they train harder than wrestlers? Of course not. Do they sacrifice more than wrestlers? No way. Are they better athletes than wrestler? C'mon. The anonymous life of a wrestler (and of any of the many unnoticed, uncelebrated sports that get their moment to shine every four years at the Olympics) never felt more unfair than it did during that long march through Olympic Stadium, standing next to the basketball stars. I never wrestle for the fame, obviously; nobody does. But I don't think I ever realized the incredible disparity in that fame and recognition until just then. I never had time to be a big sports fan, and so I never understood America's incredible fascination with team sports. I was always about the individual duals; I couldn't name three Super Bowl champions or World Series winners. But now I understood that I was in the vast minority. Goodness, some sports stars really are heroes. Not me, but some.

By the time we wound up in the middle of the stadium, I had left the American basketball players' sides and moved over to hang out with some of the wrestlers from Cuba and South America, dudes who walked my walk and spoke my language. It was then that I realized how singular that American heartbeat in me had become.

While athletes from all of these countries were nice to each other, many of them stared menacingly at me. Many of them made comments that I luckily could not hear that well. They laughed at my cap, poked jokingly at my tie, and basically treated me like the enemy.

That is another thing that Americans don't realize about the Olympics. While the Games emphasize how tight we can bond as members of one planet, they also accentuate how alone we feel as Americans sometimes. Bottom line, the rest of the world just doesn't always like us very much, and nowhere is that more evident than in the one sporting event that is supposed to hide that.

Think about it. Nobody dominates the Summer Olympics like the United States; nobody financially supports the Summer Olympics like the United States with our billion-dollar television package, yet how many times have those Olympics actually been held in the United States? In the last twenty-five years, just twice. We dominate softball and what happens? The sport is dropped from the Games. We love baseball and what happens? The sport is dropped from the Games.

The International Olympic Committee looks down on the United States, and it treats us American Olympians like we are spoiled and arrogant children, and sometimes that's true, but most of the time we are just hardworking stiffs like me. This occasionally nasty attitude toward us seeps into the entire Olympic culture, athletes from other countries shunning us, fans booing us, all of which is actually great for our team, because it gives us the necessary chip that our shoulders require to push even harder.

Except for me in Beijing. I had a chip on my shoulder already, but it was smothering me.

From the moment I climbed out of my middle seat and departed the plane after that twelve-hour commercial flight, I was in a wrestling fog. Maybe it was jet leg. Maybe it was the Beijing smog. Maybe it was the worries about cutting weight—remember that whole disaster from the beginning? Maybe it was just plain fear.

Whatever it was, for the first week of practice with my partner and brother Angel, I sucked. He was about thirty pounds bigger than me, but usually I can get out from under him. Suddenly, I couldn't. He was smarter and craftier than me, but usually I can get around him. Suddenly, no way.

Terry Brands, my Olympic Training Center coach, was concerned about my struggles in Beijing, and he should have immediately reported them to Olympic coach Kevin Jackson. But he didn't. I later discovered that he didn't want to hassle his bosses with something he figured he could fix himself.

Apparently he had reported problems with me in the past, and been told to back off and let me grow up and work it out on my own, which didn't happen. Terry even blames himself for me getting pinned in the national finals before the Olympics, because he says he saw I was struggling and was afraid to take matters into his own hands.

No more. This time he was going to handle this situation and my problems himself. This time he was going to handle me himself. Literally a couple of days before my competition, he walked into the wrestling room at Beijing Normal University, plopped down on a bench, and strapped on a pair of wrestling shoes.

"What are you doing?" I asked.

"Kicking your ass," he said.

He jumped onto the mat and grabbed for my neck and away we went, wrestling hard for nearly an hour, this forty-year-old man pounding on a twenty-one-year-old kid. Damn, he was still tough. Damn, he could still bring it. He clawed me and cursed me. He boxed my ears and twisted my neck. It was baffling, it was brutal, but it was ultimately beautiful and really really helpful.

Because by the time I finished, that fog had been lifted, my clumsiness had disappeared, my technique was back, I understood exactly what I needed to do to win an Olympic gold medal.

"Had enough?" he said after throwing my wet and drained body off the mat.

"No. I want more," I said.

"Angel, get in here," he said.

"What the hell?" I said.

And so, with no rest, fighting against my older brother, I was pounded for another hour, and now I was really ready. From that moment on, it was all about losing the weight and getting some sleep and holding the focus and . . .

Bang! Bang! Bang!

Fast-forward to six thirty a.m. of August 19, 2008.

It was the day of the Olympic 121-pound (or 55-kilogram) wrestling competition.

My time.

From the moment I had finished wrestling Terry, from the moment I knew I was ready, I walked around Beijing as if in a dream. Now, as Kevin Jackson banged on the door of my room at the Olympic Village, I was literally in a dream.

Bang! Bang! Bang!

I was dreaming of getting carried off the mat. But I wasn't being carried on a stretcher. Oh no, I was being carried, aloft in someone's arms. I was literally dreaming about winning the gold medal.

Crazy, huh? Well, you might remember my awful struggle to lose all that weight the previous day, a whole ten pounds in just a few hours. I celebrated by eating, like, five bowls of wonderfully carb-heavy pasta. Anytime I eat that much, I sleep great, like a baby. And that night, I had the best sleep of my life. So no wonder I dreamed of doing something great.

Did I really think I was going to win the gold medal? How the hell could I have known that? The last time I competed against these guys from around the world, I finished in last place, remember? Had my ass handed to me?

Bang! Bang! Bang!

"Time to go! Time to go!" shouted Jackson through the door.

I jumped up, showered quickly, went with Jackson to the cafeteria, and ate three scrambled eggs and an orange. And yes, Clarissa, afterward I threw the orange peel away. I promise. I wasn't going to mess with any bad karma on this day of all days.

The tournament was structured in five rounds, with nineteen wrestlers competing, a best-of-three-rounds format in each match. Because of a random draw, myself and nine other wrestlers had a first-round bye. So I had to win four matches, which is still like running four marathons. The draw for my first opponent had already been held, but I never like to know who I'm wrestling against until the last minute, so on the van to the China Agricultural University gym, I was pretty nervous.

When I walked into the joint and saw my name on the board, I nearly leaped for joy. My opponent was Radolsav Velikov of Bulgaria. He was the 2006 world champion. He had beat the crap out of me previously, pinned me, in another tournament about a year earlier. If I wasn't careful, this Olympic dream business would be over for me in about four freaking minutes.

"This is awful," said a nearby fan of mine.

"This is great!" I shouted.

This really was great. At least in my mind. To be the best, you've got to beat the best, so why not start right now? There was no way a last-place world finisher can win the Olympics without a ton of confidence, and there was no better way to build that confidence than by beating this guy.

This was no different than finding, challenging, and fighting the toughest guy in the wrestling room on the first day of practice. If I beat him, then everyone and everything else falls into line.

I walked happily into the warm-up room to get warm and loose with Angel, rolling around on the mat, trying different moves, stretching different parts of my body. I put on my iPod and listened to a recording of my voice talking about focusing and staying strong, mixed around with R. Kelly singing about "The World's Greatest."

All of a sudden, it was time, the match was on, my time had come, and I was walking up to the mat where Velikov was standing. I saw nothing but the back of my coach, Terry Brands.

I heard nothing but the voices in my head, from many years ago, from Coach Richard telling me that everyone hates me to Alonzo telling me that I was blowing my only chance. The voices fueled me. The walk strengthened me. When the match started, I could have wrestled all of China. I charged harder than I ever charged. Unfortunately, that left me open for a leg clinch that gave Velikov the only point of the first period. Shit. Damn. My aggressive style cost me the round, and now it could cost me my dream.

Coming off the match for my brief rest between periods, I looked into Terry's eye, and I realized that they were strangely bright. I was two minutes from ruining my life, and he was happy?

"You're doing the right thing; you're doing the right thing," he said. "He's going to get tired. You're wearing him out. Keep pushing. Keep pushing!"

By the middle of the second round, I realized he was right. I could see it in Velikov's eyes, a mixture of fear and exhaustion. I could feel it in his chest, his breath coming in quick and rapid bursts. I nailed him on a takedown to win the period and send it to the decisive third period. I came to the sidelines smiling. The guy was done. I could tell. He couldn't keep up with me. He couldn't stop me. This third period was going to be a cinch. It was going to be mine.

Or, um, wait a second, maybe not. He came out at me with one last burst of energy, and took a 2–1 lead on me, I looked up at the scoreboard and thought, Oh shit, thirty seconds left. I need to find something somewhere within me to win this.

What I found was back in a sweaty gym in Colorado Springs. What I found was back on a rocky mountain outside of Phoenix.

What I found was the hours and hours of extra work that I had used to get here, to get myself to this point.

When everyone else was toweling off, I was always doing thirty more minutes of push-ups and pull-ups and sit-ups. When everyone was watching, I was working my butt off.

"Go, horse, go!" shouted Terry, pounding the mat. "You go! You go!"

What I found was my past, brought to the present, kicking ass toward my future. Once again, someone was watching and I was working. This time that someone was Velikov, who paused just long enough for me to throw him down and score the last-gasp points to give me the round and the match.

As I staggered off the mat and into Terry's arms for a quick congratulations hug, I thought about what he said when he inspired my post-workout routines back in Colorado Springs.

"You've got to do something that nobody else in the world is doing," he told me then. "And you've got to do it every day."

It took two years and thousands of extra miles, but I finally understood the reality of exactly what he said, and why he said it. I had just beaten the toughest guy I had ever wrestled. One of the toughest guys in the world. And all of a sudden, I was three matches from one of the most unlikely gold medals the wrestling world had ever seen.

And I had all of . . . thirty minutes to savor it?

"Change your socks, change your shorts!" said Terry, walking me into this closet-sized room near the mats. "Lay down. I'll be out here."

So I lay down and pondered my next opponent. Or, at least, I tried to ponder my next opponent. Problem was, I had never heard of him. His name was Besarion Gochashvili of Georgia, and I don't mean Atlanta. He had dropped a weight class to be here. He probably thought he could overpower the little guy. Good. The iPod went back on my head, the voice of R. Kelly again filled my mind: *"I am a river, down in the valley. I am a vision, and I can see clearly."*

Before my hair even dried from the sweat from my previous fight, I was back on the mat, me and Gochashvili, and I quickly learned this guy had two things going for him.

He had a great takedown move. And he had awful body odor. He smelled like a wet dog. I'm sure it was from his diet of garlic and grease and fatty meats. Many wrestlers from his part of the country smell like him. They all make fun of American wrestlers, saying we smell like girls. They ridicule our daily use of showers. And who knows, maybe they're right, maybe we care too much about hygiene; maybe we should be more natural.

I only know one thing for certain. This Georgian stunk to the high heavens, and for the second time in these Olympics, a smell distracted me, but not as much as that takedown move, which gave him a win in the first period, and put me back on the ropes.

"What the hell!" I screamed at Brands on the sideline.

"A matter of time," Brands said again. "He cannot hang with you. Keep charging, horse. Go, go, go!"

How could he be so calm when my entire career was going down the smelly tubes? For a second straight match, I was moments from extinction, yet Terry was acting like I was on the verge of a championship. I didn't know where he got his confidence in me, but I knew I needed to grab on to it and let him help me believe in myself.

Well, once again, he knew. He knew me better than I knew myself at that moment. I kept charging, and soon Gochashvili started retreating. I nailed him with a takedown and a gut wrench, dominating and winning the period, and I knew it was done. This one fight was finally over. I knew because in the middle of the match at the end of the period, this smelly dog's head started bobbing up and down, up and down.

I had seen that happen to the old and malnourished strays that would hang around the Phoenix barrio. Their raggedy heads would bob up and down, up and down, and then they would find a corner, crawl into it, and finally lay down their heads and die. Which is exactly what happened here. In the third period, Gochashvili could barely move, and I scored on two takedowns and an ankle lace for a 3–0 victory that gave me the match.

"You see?" shouted Terry, walking with me off the mat. "Do you see?"

I saw my arms, which, despite having wrestled the two most important matches of my life in a span of an hour, hung by my sides, strangely enough, still strong.

I saw my legs, which should have been rubber, purposely carrying me to the warm-up room as if they were two strong oaks.

I saw what I thought was a miracle.

Lord, I'm smack in the middle of an Olympic wrestling marathon, and I wasn't even tired. My adrenaline must've been racing because even after those epic early fights, I was still going strong.

Lord, someone was in for a beating.

"I'm that star up in the sky, I'm that mountain peak up high."

Thirty minutes spent resting back in a little room off the wrestling room, and one power bar and one half an orange later, I prepared to walk out for my semifinal match when I heard the most surprising sound coming from my duffel bag.

It was my Beijing cell phone ringing, ringing, ringing. Who could it be? Who could possibly be calling me at that moment? An old friend from the barrio proudly calling with some timeless advice? An old coach from Colorado Springs tearfully calling with some last-minute pep talk? Or maybe it was the guy who owned that junkyard that we lived in back in Arizona?

This would be a great spot in my story to insert some amazing drama that came from that call. But, aw, hell, to tell you the truth, I was just too focused on kicking somebody's butt, the next person's butt, and I never even answered it!

"Easy," said Terry, grabbing me before I took the mat. "Easy."

Why easy? Because my opponent was hardheaded Namig Sevdimov of Azerbaijan. He was a former European champion who had beaten me last year.

He was the kind of guy who would poke me in the eye, throw an elbow into my head, little stuff that could make me blow up. Terry knew that if I wasn't careful, if I didn't take it easy and cool down a bit, I could lose my temper and then the match.

I was fine. I was fine. I was . . . Wait a minute, that son of a bitch! Moments into the match he was all over me, taking advantage of my calm attitude to push me around the mat and score five points and wipe me out, winning the round.

For the third straight match, I was on the ropes. For the third time in one morning, I was on the verge of seeing my last four years go to waste.

"I want to kill this guy!" I told Terry as we talked in between rounds.

"Remember why you're here!" Terry replied. "Forget about fighting and start wrestling! Bring the heat! Bring the heat!"

Thousands of times I've heard Terry yell that same phrase to me in the wrestling room: "Bring the heat." I've had to change focus fast after flunking classes at school, or fighting with Clarissa, or fretting about the loneliness and being so far from home.

Did I know how to turn it on? Easy. Could I turn it on quickly? In a second. Sevdimov realized this in the second period, when I was on him like a scratchy blanket. I scored the first takedown and kept pushing until I won the period, bringing us to the third and deciding period.

"He's tired. He's tired; you've got him!" shouted Terry.

But I didn't believe it. This ornery guy, while clearly exhausted, was also clearly angry enough to make somebody pay. He reminded me of someone whose heart is as big as their neck, a wrestler who would not quit until he was peeled from the mat. You know what? He kind of reminded me of me.

Sure enough, we fought evenly for nearly all three minutes of the match, and it was tied at 3–3 all with twenty-four seconds left when I glanced at the scoreboard, at the crowd, at Terry, and was hit with an instantaneous thought.

Mexican ice cream. I once fought my ass off for Mexican ice cream. I once fought for a drunk's respect, a gang member's mercy, a barrio's admiration, a mother's love, and Mexican ice cream.

I won those fights for my life back then. I can sure as hell win a fight for a piece of metal right now. Sevdimov never saw the move that hit him, a single-leg takedown that gave me the round and the match in the final moment.

Kevin Jackson, my Olympic coach, grabbed me and lifted me in the air as if I were already a champion. Sevdimov looked down as if he had just lost all respect for himself.

The pro-Azerbaijan crowd was booing in disappointment. Sevdimov's coach was fuming. I walked over to him and stuck out my hand for the traditional post-match handshake, but, as you can see on the video, he slapped my hand away in an international insult. That prick. I was done being nice, and I was going to go crazy now, no more Mr. Nice Guy, enough of taking the hard knocks, I was going to kick this guy's ass and . . .

I didn't. Nobody told me not to, but I didn't anyway. I wanted to slap him. I wanted to flip the bird to the crowd. I wanted to lose it in front of people who wouldn't judge me if they only realized the desperation that filled me. But I didn't react. I didn't do anything. I just walked off the mat and headed to the vans to go back to Beijing Normal to rest for my gold medal match several hours later.

Four years ago, if I felt someone had insulted me like that, I would have attacked that person and lashed out, my temper flaring. But I guess something had finally happened to me after all that time. After I had been plucked from the barrio and after I had been placed in the Olympic Training Center and after I had been forced to become accountable for my actions and trained to be the best.

I guess what happened is that I finally grew up. I grew up to channel my aggression and hone my skills and understand my surroundings and take my life to where, right now, driving through the crowded streets of Beijing, I was six minutes from an Olympic gold medal.

I grew up, and it was the United States of America that raised me.

Gawd, I loooove this country.

★ NINE ★

"Man, this shit came so fast."

The thought rolled around in my head as my body rolled around in the bed.

"Man, how did this happen?"

My life passed before my eyes as Terry Brands' sheets bunched up under my body.

It was the early afternoon on August 19, 2008. I had returned to the USA Wrestling team's Beijing Normal University headquarters after winning my first three matches in the 121-pound (or 55-kilogram) division of 2008 Olympic freestyle wrestling. I had about four hours to rest before the gold-medal match. My body was quivering. My mind was racing. I needed sleep. My coach, Terry Brands, ushered me into his room and told me to use his bed and get some rest.

"Man, who pushed the fast-forward button on my life?"

I lay on top of the covers in my shorts and T-shirt while Terry turned out the lights. I told him I wanted it dark, and suddenly it was completely dark, but damn it, I could never sleep in the dark, remember? I lay there and tried to lose myself in the blackness but all I was losing was my mind.

"Man, what did I do to deserve this?"

I couldn't stop thinking about my journey. I couldn't stop thinking about the impossibility of that journey. This just doesn't happen. I mean, this just never happens, not even in the United States of America, not even in the movies, not even in my dreams.

"Oh my God, am I dreaming?"

I sat up suddenly, walked over, and turned on the lights. I looked at myself in a mirror and I touched the shiner under my right eye. I touched the welts on my face. I grabbed my cauliflower ear. You know, I can't feel that ear. I'll never be able to feel that ear. Thank God, because sometimes it's the only thing on my body that doesn't hurt.

Yes, this was me. Okay, I recognized this kid peering back at me in the mirror. This was the kid whose mother and father snuck into a country that he now represented in one of the greatest competitions in the world. This was the kid who fought to survive in a country that later today will dress him up and hug him and cheer like hell for him to bring them back a gold medal. To bring them honor.

"I'm not supposed to be here, am I?"

The air-conditioning hummed on high. The sheets were cool to the touch. But I was burning up. I was on fire. I was feverish with disbelief and fear. I stripped down to my underwear, climbed back into bed, and lay there in a thick, nervous sweat.

I thought first about my mother, the strong and beautiful

Nelly Rico, how she never let us know we were homeless, never let us be ashamed that we were poor, and never, ever allowed us to give up. I was furious that she couldn't be here with me. I pounded the pillow and screamed out her name and cursed her absence from these Games.

My mother had long since been granted amnesty and given a green card that allowed her to remain in the United States. But she still couldn't travel overseas because she didn't have a passport. She didn't qualify for a U.S. passport, and she could never afford to return to Mexico to pick up a Mexican passport.

So she could not come to Beijing to watch the biggest moment of my life. I rolled over, hugged that same pillow, and wished desperately it was her. I sat up in bed and wondered what she was doing right now. I wondered if she had been able to watch any of my three previous matches. It was after midnight in the United States, and again, I wondered what she was doing at this exact moment while I was halfway around the world.

Turns out, she had been doing plenty. At around ten p.m. back home, my first matches were being shown on the cable channel MSNBC. There is no cable TV in the Colorado Springs apartment where she had moved a year earlier to share with my brother Angel and other family members, so my mother and some relatives and friends donned T-shirts with a giant CEJUDO printed on them and drove over to the Hurtados' house.

Dave Hurtado was in Beijing with me for support, but his wife, Dianne, had stayed home with their daughter, so there was somebody at the house to host visitors.

Which turned out to be a good thing, because my mom never called first to tell them they were coming over. Apparently, she never even asked if anybody was going to be home. Figuring the Hurtados were like family, her posse just pulled up at their house two hours before midnight without warning.

Turns out, though, other Hurtado neighbors and friends had done the same thing, so the house was filled with people watching me, crowded around their television. My mother was embraced and welcomed into the home and offered the prime viewing area for the match.

"No, no," she said, pointing to the kitchen. "I'll sit in there."

"But there is no television in the kitchen," she was told.

"I know," she said.

She was still too nervous to watch me wrestle in big competitions. It had been that way during the few times she was ever able to come to my matches back home, where she would pace outside the gym or stroll around the concourse. I never thought it would keep her from watching me wrestle in the Olympics. But then, I always underestimated her fear and concern for her youngest boy.

That's my mom. I guess the consistency that helped us survive is the same kind of consistency that still makes her sick with nervousness every time she watches me wrestle. So while she drove all the way over to the Hurtados' house to watch me compete in the Olympics, she didn't actually watch me. Instead, she waited in the Hurtados' kitchen throughout all three matches, figuring out how I was doing by listening for the cheers coming from the other room. When the first three matches were finished, there was a long break before the gold-medal match, which wouldn't air until about four a.m., so she went home, leaving everyone wondering how she would ever find out that night if I won gold.

"Is this really me?"

After thinking about my mom, I then thought about my brothers and sisters, how they taught me to laugh, to love and, most of all, to fight. All those afternoons spent throwing couch cushions at each other. All those broken doors and busted cabinets. All those nights sleeping side by side by side by side by side by side by side. Dang, I missed those nights, and even though Gloria and Alonzo and, of course, Angel would be in the Beijing bleachers today, I missed them all terribly because I had been so focused on this goal and hadn't had time to hang out with them and discuss the journey I'd been on.

"What if this is all a joke?"

Then I sat up in bed, reached into a drawer, and pulled out Terry's Bible. He always had a Bible. "I know what side my bread is buttered on," he would say. I never much read the Bible besides that first time at the Olympic Training Center, when it was my only source of entertainment and distraction. I never much cared for church, except maybe for the free food afterward. But I prayed. They were often prayers of desperation, praying for a ride home in the rain or a sandwich in the afternoon, but they were prayers nonetheless.

I opened the Bible to a random page and started reading. I would be lying if I told you I remembered what I read that day in Beijing. I only remembered the thick feel of the book, the solidity of it in my hands, and the solemn texture of the pages, and how the words perplexed me. There was so much more to life than wrestling. There were so many more important steps to take in life. I always thought I was somehow supposed to win that gold medal, but maybe not. Maybe the next step in my path would begin with a loss. Maybe God wanted me to spread His word through my sportsmanship and composure in the face of defeat. Maybe God wanted to teach me a lesson about only going to His house for the free doughnuts. I thought the Bible would fill me with answers, but instead it only gave me more questions.

"God, would you just please tell me what to do?"

I put the book down, rolled over, and thought about angels, about all the people who had touched my life and brought me to this point.

I thought about Frank Saenz, the crusty old inner-city Phoenix coach who rescued me from the Mexican ice-cream men and taught me my first wrestling skills. I thought about Tracy Greiff, my mentor and protector and friend, a man who saw me only as a scrawny little kid with a need, a man who answered my calls even when nobody knew my name. I thought about Dave Hurtado, my father in Colorado Springs. I thought about Eric Albarracin, a guy who took me under his giant wing at the Olympic Training Center, teaching me about women and life. I thought about too many people to name here, people who once took pity on this poor, strangely towheaded kid, people who probably never had any idea they were making an investment in a potential Olympic gold medalist. Neither did I.

"How can I ever pay everybody back?"

I sat up in bed again and started to sing. If my mother were here, she would be singing me to sleep, so I figured I could do it myself. I picked a song that was covered by the popular Latin group Mana.

I softly crooned, *"Se no te hubieras ido . . ."*

The English translation is, "If you hadn't left . . ."

Yes, at last, I was thinking about my father. Only through his death could I have had this new, remarkable, revitalized life. He was sometimes a bad man, but he was always my man, my papa, and only by washing myself in the dust of his grave could I bury my pain and focus on his redemption, his redemption through me. Whatever happened in a couple of hours was going to happen in honor of his memory. He may have tried to hurt me, knowingly or unknowingly, at one time. But while he is forever gone from me, he will always be in me. And I can hold on to the good things I remember, rather than all the bad stuff.

"Isn't it time to get up yet?"

The dark didn't work, the Bible hadn't worked, the singing hadn't worked—it was the worst four hours of my life, lying wide-awake in a strange bed in my underwear, wondering whether I deserved what was about to happen to me.

I finally climbed out of bed, stepped into the shower, got dressed in my sweats, and walked outside to find Terry.

"How did you sleep?" asked my coach.

"Uh, great," I lied.

Waiting for us outside was a limousine. I had never been in a limousine before. I wish I could have enjoyed it. But I was too busy thinking about the previous five hours, and starting to worry about the next sixty minutes.

I found out that my opponent was going to be an Asian champion, Tomihiro Matsunaga of Japan. He had defeated defending world champion Besik Kudukhov of Russia in the semifinals. Several U.S. officials were watching that match on TV as we were leaving the arena five hours earlier, and they all cheered when Matsunaga pulled the upset, and that sort of freaked me out.

After all I had been through that day already, did they really think I couldn't beat a defending world champion like Kudukhov? And if Matsunaga was good enough to win that match, why couldn't he win the gold? I hadn't been the certain win, and neither was he. So we were the same.

Some folks will say I got a lucky draw. I say that at this point, at that level, there is no such thing as luck. I was scared of Matsunaga in a way that I thought my previous three opponents had not been scared of me. He beat Kudukhov. He could beat me.

Then we arrived at the arena and went to the warm-up area. I leaned over to tie up my wrestling shoes and . . . suddenly that fear disappeared. Suddenly, all the tension from the previous five hours lifted off my back. Suddenly, I thought to myself, Damn, I am going to win this gold medal!

It was the shoes. I know it was the shoes. Remember how my first pair of wrestling shoes were a pair of scuffed dogs given to me by some rich kid that I had beaten? I won the match, but I was the one who was embarrassed. Remember how Frank Saenz used to give me used wrestling shoes out of a giant box, like a Goodwill donation? Those shoes never fit, and I never felt right. Remember when Angel and I had one pair of wrestling shoes between us? I would wear wrestling shoes one day, he would wear the tennis shoes, then the next day we'd trade? Every other day, I felt small and embarrassed.

But now I had my own shoes, beautiful blue wrestling shoes with red and white trim. They fit tightly, and they laced perfectly. I know it's a simple thing, but I saw these shoes and thought, You know, I worked like hell for these. I sweated buckets for these, and I gave everything up for these. I earned these. I deserve these. And I deserve this chance to go out there and wrestle my ass off and bring home a gold medal.

This moment was not given to me, dammit, I took it. And right here, right now, I'm going to own it forever.

I turned to Terry as we walked toward the mat.

"It's ours," I said.

"What did you say?" he said incredulously.

"I got this kid," I said.

"You better make sure," he said.

"I've never been more sure of anything in my life," I said.

I walked to the mat and briefly looked up and saw a dozen family members and friends standing in the corner bleachers. I flashed them a quick smile. Not all of them were smiling back at me. I later learned that, in typical Cejudo fashion, a brawl had just nearly broken out.

The problem was, throughout the day, none of them had wanted to sit down while I wrestled. They figured that they had traveled thousands of miles to see their homey, so they wanted to really see him, get a good look at him down on the floor there. Eric wanted to stand. Alonzo wanted to stand. Angel wanted to stand. All of them wanted to stand.

Nobody behind them was really complaining. The crowd actually loved watching the crazy American family with painted faces and banners jumping up and down, cheering for their favorite son and causing a happy ruckus. But the Chinese security guards were apparently not used to this. They were apparently not used to such open signs of love and affection and, okay, nuttiness and wild energy. So they surrounded my family and continually urged them politely to sit down and be quiet. And urged. And urged. Soon, I guess, it seemed like the entire Chinese army had my family and friends surrounded, trying to get them to calm down. But the Cejudo clan didn't move—they wouldn't move and they wouldn't sit down and they certainly weren't leaving.

"We didn't want to get thrown out, but if your little bro is down there, what are you going to do?" Alonzo told the newspapers later.

My family stood firm and won their fight. And soon, quickly, faster than I ever imagined, I won mine.

From the start, Matsunaga looked nervous and scared, like he had something to lose. I had nothing to lose, and like always, I wrestled like it. I made an aggressive mistake in the beginning that gave him a point, but I just kept coming, the street fighter on the main stage. And late in the first period, I fooled him by motioning toward his left leg then diving into his right leg. It was enough to spin him on his back for a two-point move. The round ended up tied 2–all, but because I had the higher-scoring move, I was officially the round winner. Figures, huh? What worked me throughout my life just kept working for me. I was given points not only for skill, but hunger.

Not much was said during the thirty seconds between rounds. Not much needed to be said. Terry looked in my eyes and he knew. I looked in my heart and I knew. It all came down to this.

Nine seconds. That's all it took for me to win the second round and clinch the gold. Nine freaking seconds is all it took for me to dive to his right leg and throw him to his back in the best high-crotch takedown of my entire career. The perfect high-crotch takedown. The approximately one millionth high-crotch takedown. It is a move I had been doing hundreds of times a week for four years in practice. I could do it in my sleep. Now I just did it in my dream.

The move scored three points, and those three points held up until the horn sounded for the end of the round, the end of match, the end of my journey. Matsunaga fell to his back in pain. I dropped to my knees in tears.

I knew it would happen, but I couldn't believe it actually happened when it did. I knew I deserved to win, but I couldn't fathom myself as a winner in that moment. Really and truly. I stood up, briefly raised my arms, and ran weeping into the arms of Kevin Jackson, who then carried me over to Terry Brands. I hugged Terry for what seemed like forever, and also for what felt like not nearly long enough. I walked to the center of the ring and, holding my left hand over my face to scoop up the tears, I extended my right hand to Matsunaga in congratulations.

And here came the American flag. In a tightly wrapped package, incredibly, it had been thrown halfway across the gym by my bandanna-wearing buddy Eric Albarracin, who risked arrest for doing so, but who didn't care.

"Henry, if they stopped me from throwing it, I was going to just climb the wall and run it over to you myself," he said later. "Without that flag, you were just another dude in a leotard."

With the stars and stripes in my hands, I felt like the American Superman. My mother had coveted this flag so much; she risked her life to live in its shadow. During my moment of triumph, the least I could do was take it dancing.

I wrapped that flag around my shoulder and I flew. From one end of the mat to another, the wings of my youth now the wings of my victory. I was flying, flying, flying. Then I was collapsing on the mat, the weight of my sobbing throwing me down, the protective blanket of my youth now covering me once more, dabbing away my thick tears, warming my trembling body.

God bless America. Land that I love. After holding the flag close to my heart, moments later I stood respectfully on the podium as they raised it to the sky, my sides too sore from crying to sing, and my heart still pumping too fast to think. So I just stood there, standing straight up and basking in what will surely forever be the greatest honor of my life.

The flag wasn't honoring me. I was honoring the flag. The victory wasn't just mine alone, though. The victory was ours. All of ours. From the black bars of south-central Los Angeles to the old railroad inclines of Colorado, from immigrant fishermen's homes in Maine to immigrant cowboy ranches in New Mexico, from Wall Street to Main Street, from brown to black to white, from red to white to blue, this was about all of us.

If Henry Cejudo could win a gold medal, well, then, what the hell, we all won gold medals.

Including the woman holed up in a Colorado Springs bathroom in the middle of the night. That would be my mom. That is where she watched me win my gold medal. I am not making this up.

After leaving the Hurtado home, my mom and several family members stayed awake for several hours in hopes of finding out the results of my gold-medal match on the family computer. Remember, they didn't have cable TV. My mother ordered someone to bang on that keyboard until the match came up online, and somehow, it did. To this day, I don't know which Web site carried the video of the match, and she doesn't either.

They were all crowded around the small monitor for the start of the match when suddenly my mother decided that, even tiny and digitally, she couldn't stand to watch me fight. So she left the room and went into the bathroom, returning only sporadically to check on scores she didn't understand in a sport she doesn't really comprehend.

"Is he winning?" she would shout.

"We think so!" they would report back.

Finally, from the bathroom, she heard wild cheering in front of the computer, the wildest cheering of this wildest of nights. She rushed out and on the tiny video playing on the tiny computer screen, she saw Kevin Jackson picking me up and she knew.

"Henry won!" she shouted, jumping up and down in those thick shoes that paved my way. "Henry won!"

Only, nobody in the family understood her or the words coming out of her mouth. It wasn't because she was speaking Spanish; it was because her throat was strangely thick and her eyes were strangely wet.

"Oh my God," said one of her friends. "Are you crying?"

Despite enduring a lifetime of heartache, that night was the first time Nelly Rico had ever shed a tear in public.

"He won!" she kept shouting, and crying, clear through until morning, her strange and wonderful tears making the journey from darkness to dawn, as the sun rose in the United States. "He won!"

★ TEN ★

Five ounces.

A dozen years of sweat for five ounces.

Did you know that was the weight of an Olympic gold medal? Five measly ounces?

Did you also know that the gold medal isn't really gold? It's actually 92.5 percent silver with a gold coating. On the street, without any meaning or sentiment involved, it would sell for about one hundred and fifty dollars.

Around my neck, though, that sucker was huge and priceless and powerful. I learned that quickly after my Olympic victory. Took all of about five minutes.

As I left the medal podium and was walking out of the arena, I saw my family and friends crowding around the railing just above the tunnel. They couldn't get past security to reach me. I didn't have time to walk all the way back through the arena to get up to them. So, brandishing my medal like a golden ticket,

I turned to one of the security guards and pointed to the cheering crowd above.

"I'm going in!" I shouted.

And with that, I climbed up against the rail and leaned into the stands and hugged everyone in sight. I felt the tears of my sister Gloria, the sweat of my old coach Frank Saenz, the hard embrace of Eric Albarracin, the long hug of my brothers Angel and Alonzo, the heartbeat of my past smothering me with love.

By the time I had climbed down, I was left completely moved and speechless, which wasn't real good timing, because now it was time for the traditional post-match press conference. If you notice, I haven't really written much about the media so far here because, well, the media had never written much about me.

Wrestling is not a big spectator sport, so the mainstream newspapers and writers rarely cover us. Throw in the fact that I'm a little guy from the streets, and even the media that wrote about wrestling rarely focused on me.

There was a guy in Phoenix, Norm Frauenheim, who did a tremendous job following me through high school. The guy is one of the best sportswriters in the country, a real legend. Then there was a guy from Denver, Benjamin Hochman, one of the best young sportswriters in the country, who did some cool stuff on me at the Olympic Training Center. It was Hochman who perfectly captured my first confident public statement about the Olympics, recording a quote that I used as my inspiration. I was sitting with him after a practice one day when the words to describe my goals just popped out.

"That yellow butter medal . . . it's on the podium waiting for someone to take it," I told him.

A yellow butter medal? Where in the hell did I come up with

that? I have no idea. Probably from thinking about the buttered tortillas that I ate as a kid. Whatever. I love that quote, and I will always remember Hochman for printing it perfectly.

But besides those two writers, nobody really followed me regularly. I didn't do many interviews, so going into a loud and all of a sudden crowded gold-medal press conference, I felt like the Cowardly Lion walking into that wizard's forest.

Strange sights everywhere, huge cameras and tiny recorders and bright lights and boom mikes and all shapes and sizes of writers, oh my. Everyone crammed into a small room, and everyone staring at me and my left eye and my scarred face and my sweaty body. They started shouting questions and I didn't have any time to think, any time to prepare. I had no choice but to answer from the heart.

"I'm living the American dream!" I said.

Next question.

"The United States is the land of opportunity and I'm so glad I can represent it," I said.

Next question.

"I might just sleep with this," I said of the medal.

I thought American writers were supposed to be tough, but these guys seemed as thrilled as I was that I was holding the medal. It was weird, but from the red in their cheeks and eyes, it looked like some of them had even been crying. As I later learned, some of them actually had been crying.

This was all very strange considering, just two hours before my gold-medal match, most of the American writers had never even heard of me. Nobody thought I would even have a chance at a gold medal, so nobody bothered to check me out.

The writers only heard about me when they received a mass

e-mail from the USA Olympic folks in the early afternoon announcing that I had reached the gold medal match. Even then, they only barely knew my story, but a potential gold was a gold nonetheless, and an unknown gold was a good story, so about a dozen American writers climbed on a bus that took them from the press center to the wrestling arena.

Once there, the writers were swarmed by the great USA Wrestling publicity team of Gary Abbott and Craig Sesker. The writers were given a small *Sports Illustrated* story about me that had been done earlier, and directed to stories by Frauenheim and Hochman, and then Abbott and Sesker filled in the gaps about my history, stats, and training.

Thanks to Abbott and Sesker, by the time I took the mat for the gold match, all the writers finally knew the basis of my story, my crazy journey to that point. So when I won the gold medal, a bunch of them were actually crying along with me, moved after hearing how far I'd come, and how high I'd reached.

All of which also moved me so much that I didn't want our interview session to end. These guys really seemed to understand me. And so I couldn't shut up; I was so excited, so happy that I had reached so many people and that my story finally meant something to so many people outside my normal orbit. I spilled whatever bits of my guts were still intact, telling them as much as I could about my background, my struggles and, of course, my mother.

I loved talking about my mother. But I must admit, I was initially embarrassed enough by her situation such that nobody in my family wanted to share the details with anyone.

"Why isn't she here?" the writers asked.

"She gets too nervous," I said.

"She had to stay home and babysit," Angel said.

"She doesn't like to travel," Alonzo said.

Lies, lies, lies. The truth was, of course, that my mother didn't go to the Olympics because she didn't have a passport. While everyone knew that she had long since been granted amnesty and could work in the United States, the fact that she couldn't even leave the country to watch her son wrestle for the Olympics was a harsh reminder of her past sin—the only sin being that of an immigrant, a former illegal newcomer to this country—and I hated it.

So I lied at the first press conference, and I lied at the next couple of interviews, and I was going to keep twisting the truth about my mom's situation until Sesker pulled me aside.

"Dude, don't be ashamed of the truth," he said. "You are the American dream, and part of that dream is your mother's situation, and addressing it will only make people respect you more."

As usual, Sesker was right, and from that moment, I told only the truth. From that moment, I realized that my truth was not embarrassing, it was redeeming. I understood that my truth, while often ugly, had led me to a place of unrefined beauty.

It's sort of like storm clouds, you know? They can hang there in the sky all day, nasty and foreboding and pouring rain, until they begin lifting at sunset. Then they are breathtaking, purple and majestic. And even before that, while they're pounding the earth with hard rain during the long day, that rain is still nourishing—through the darkness and wet drops, fruit will eventually be born and grass will grow. That's my journey, from dark clouds to a blessed, glorious sunset, and I've learned to embrace even its most thunderous, frightening moments. What wonderful crops have grown from that initial storm, what beautiful sunsets I've seen since the clouds lifted.

It is in this same vein of honesty that I now acknowledged my most pressing thought as I finally walked away from my first post-match press conference, exhilarated and exhausted.

Where do I have to go to do the pee?

Normally, this would not even be a thought, much less a negative thought, but I was being led to the post-match drug test that is required of all gold medalists, which means I had to quickly summon up a cupful of pee. With my body completely dehydrated. With some weird dude checking out my package. Nice way to bring a champion back to earth, huh?

I often wondered why they didn't drug test *before* matches. Hell, in the thirty minutes before a match, I have to pee about a dozen times from all the water I'm drinking to stay hydrated through the wrestling and from all the nervousness before stepping onto the mat. Why don't they come to the athlete when they are all charged up and ready to stream? Why do they wait until the body is spent and the urge to pee is gone and all I want to do is collapse?

I left the huge media crowd and walked into this small, quiet room and rolled down my singlet and held the cup up to my equipment and . . . nothing. It didn't help that an Olympic drug official was standing there, making sure that the pee was actually coming from my body. Funny how I wasn't afraid to run around in a tight leotard in front of millions of people, but I was deathly afraid of peeing in front of another man.

That, and I just didn't have any pee. So I waited. And waited.

And waited. I thought about a childhood trick where you can put a sleeping person's hand in warm water and they would wet the bed. So I excused myself, walked over the sink, filled it with warm water, and dunked my head under. And waited. And waited. And still nothing.

Back at the cup, I finally did what any American man does during these times of urinary tension. I closed my eyes and thought about rain. Sheets of rain. Gutters splatting and sidewalks puddling and front porches dripping. Goodness, I nearly had to pee while coming up with those last three sentences.

Of course, it worked. Finally. Whether you're at the front of a long line at a baseball game or standing next to your boss at one of the two company urinals, thinking about rain always makes a man pee. And so I did, triumphantly finishing my task about an hour after it started.

"What the hell were you doing in there?" asked Sesker when I finally emerged.

"Singing in the rain," I told him.

My gold medal could not get me out of that drug test, which, of course, I passed. Anyone could look at my scrawny body and know that I have no use for steroids.

My gold medal then went right back to work, as I walked to the curb to climb into a waiting van to drive to my second round of interviews.

"Wait a minute, this van is not going to work," I said.

"It's not big enough for you?" said one official with a smile.

"No," I said, deadly serious. "It's not big enough for *them*."

At that moment, I pointed to what instantly became the largest Olympic celebration posse in history. All my family, all my friends, they had been with me for fifteen years of struggle, and they were going to be with me during my fifteen minutes of fame. And I didn't care if the Olympic people had to bring out a freaking bus to carry them all.

"Why can't all of them come with me to the interviews?" I asked, clutching my gold medal in my hand like that golden ticket.

"Well, uh, okay," said an official, agreeing to the madness.

And just like that, three vans appeared, and everyone piled in, and away we went, just like the old days, about ten people to a car, everyone laughing and joking. I had called shotgun, and I was riding in the front passenger seat with all sorts of arms and heads hanging over my shoulder, when I finally took a deep breath and did the one thing I had wanted to do for the last hour. Actually, it is the one thing I had wanted to do my entire life.

I phoned home to tell my mother I was an Olympic champion.

Of course she already knew. I could tell because when she answered the phone, she was weeping.

"Mama, we did it!" I shouted.

"No, no, no, *you* did it," she said between sobs.

I realized then, it was the first time I had ever heard my mother cry. She never cried when we were homeless. She snarled. She never cried when we were hungry. She growled. When our father stole our Christmas presents, she took us for haircuts instead of spending time weeping. When our electricity was turned off, she fed us cold tamales. Failure was something my mother attacked with a familiar ferocity.

Success, well, she could barely handle it. When she finally calmed down, typical Mom, her good wishes were brief and her warnings were severe.

"Congratulations, Henry," she said. "But be careful."

"Careful of what?" I said.

"This medal can make you, or it can break you," she said.

"What do you mean?" I said.

"This medal can be a blessing, or a curse . . . It's up to you to make it a blessing," she said.

"Um, okay, Mom," I said, not realizing something so beautiful could contain even one gram of evil or trouble.

"One more thing," she said.

"Anything," I said.

"Find a Christian church and thank God," she said.

"A Christian church?" I said. "In China?"

I eventually found that church, later that week, falling to my knees in thanks for this incredible gift, vowing to return the favor by helping other people realize their own gifts.

But before I paid a visit to God, I saw Michael Phelps. He was, of course, the star of the 2004 and 2008 Olympic Games, the swimmer who won a record eight gold medals in Beijing. After he returned home, all that hardware was tarnished when he was photographed apparently smoking from a bong. But I didn't know that part of him. He was my hero, and judging by the way he grabbed me and shook my hand, maybe I was his hero. Nah.

It was at this party that I realized, once again, the power of the medal. I was in a corridor when somebody realized what I was wearing, and instantly I was crushed by about one hundred people wanting to touch it. For ten minutes, I couldn't move. Except for the fact that my nostrils were filled with the scent of perfume and not dead fish, I could have been trapped on the mat under some huge Romanian. It required a giant duffel bag and a serious push by my mentor, Tracy Greiff, to extricate me from the mess, and from that day forward, I mostly carried my medal in my pocket.

Except for that first night, of course. True to my word, I slept with it around my neck. Slobbered on it and everything. It could have choked me, I guess, but it would have been much better than being choked by a sibling's arm.

No, no, I didn't also sleep with my now-famous flag. In fact, I didn't even keep the flag. During our first-night interview stops, I grew tired of carrying it, and I worried that I would drop it, so I gave it to Sesker to hold for me. And well, that's what happened. For the next three months. Yep, he stuck it in his briefcase and forgot about it and three months later, probably one of the most famous American flags in the 2008 Olympics, which was chock full of them, was still in there, in a briefcase in a basement office in an aging Colorado Springs building. I finally came by and picked it up and it's now in my mom's house. I don't know when or if I'll ever fly it again. I know for sure that I'll never fly *in it* again.

The other highlight of that first night was the unexpected speech made by Terry Brands. We were at the USA House after the match, a converted office space that was turned into a giant living room and bar, a place where Olympic medal winners hang out. It was there that Brands was given this rare coach's award for guiding me to victory. You know that Olympic coaches don't get medals for all their hard work, right? Well, Terry deserved one, and this was his time to accept the applause that goes with it. I had no idea how much it meant to him. Once he received the award, I quickly found out. He was nearly crying when he spoke, really emotional, talking about his pride in me and my effort, talking about how hard we had worked up to that point. It was obvious that his failure to match his two world champion-ships with a deserved Olympic championship really hurt. It was clear that while I was making my unexpected Olympic journey, Terry was making his own journey as well. I know there are many times I resented Terry Brands for kicking my butt and pushing me so hard, but watching him reveal himself and his overwhelmed emotions that night, I truly loved him. He did have a heart. And who knew that it beat in time with mine? A wres-tler's heart.

The second morning, I was awakened early and put right back on the interview trail. I did the *Today Show, Good Morning America, ABC World News Tonight* in a parking lot with thousands of Chi-nese crowding the fences and screaming at me.

A couple of interviewers mispronounced my name like every wrestling public address announcer in America has mis-pronounced my name. Another interviewer said, "Wow, you've got a black eye and a gold medal!"

Some people would have grown weary of this, but I thought it was great. Somebody actually asking me something that didn't start with the words "Who are you?" Somebody screaming at me in words that didn't involve cursing? For years, walking out of all those wrestling rooms in the middle of the night, I would see only myself in the cracked and cloudy mirrors. Now, all my mir-rors were filled with smiling and cheering people, standing behind me chanting my name. Every moment felt new. Every moment felt energizing. Like an entire day of Christmas pres-ents that nobody was going to steal. Of course, remember, back in Los Angeles and Las Cruces, there were times when I would get weary and distracted and break my lone Christmas present. And after long stretches of these interviews, I started feeling the same way.

Before an appearance on *Access Hollywood,* I was getting tired, so Tracy came up to me with one of two post-Olympic pep talks I received that day. He pointed to a dude who had been following us around, and whispered into my ear.

"Henry, that's one of Jay Leno's producers; he's scouting you for an appearance on the *Tonight Show,*" he said. "Show him what you've got."

Leno? The *Tonight Show?* The object of my junkyard dreams? Are you kidding me?

I walked in front of the cameras and started laughing and joking and doing everything but singing. I had a shot at Leno, and I wasn't going to screw this up. The folks at *Access Hollywood* thought I was an entertaining guy, but little did they know I was also an auditioning guy.

Two stops at McDonald's later, I was sitting in the green room for this other TV show, and I swear I can't remember which one, but I know I was getting grouchy and complaining about the time and glaring at this happy-looking guest sitting across from me.

It was that this point that Sesker leaned over and gave me that second pep talk.

"Don't you know who that woman is?" he whispered. "That's Lolo Jones. She was supposed to win the one-hundred-meter hurdles, but she hit a hurdle and finished seventh and was last seen pounding the track in disgust."

"So?" I said.

"So nobody has more reason to be upset than her, but look at her attitude," he said.

"So?" I said.

"So quit your bitching!" he said.

Oh. Okay. Like most things Sesker says, that made sense, so I quit complaining and went on this show and made everyone happy and it was all good. I think it was then that I realized, while striving for a gold medal is an individual thing, winning a gold medal is a community thing. Suddenly, my story wasn't just about me. Suddenly, my story was about all of us, and because of that, I had a responsibility to share it with others.

I was so charged up after Sesker's reminder that, while in the van going to our next interview, I did a phone interview with some tiny radio station in Miami that had somehow found USA Wrestling's cell number. They called, I answered, I spoke, and why not?

I was so fired up that after all my interviews, while taking a cab with Sesker back to the Olympic Village, I pulled out that gold medal and hung my head out the window and shouted to the crowds of Chinese folks on the sidewalks.

"Gold medal!" I said. "I did it! I did it! Thank you! Thank you!"

I didn't do much for the final couple of days of the Olympics, at least nothing that I can write here. I will only say this: All the stories about the wild partying that occurs in the Olympic Village are not accurate.

Those stories are an understatement.

From the moment I returned to the village with my medal,

my eyes were opened to what basically amounted to the ultimate love den. Beautiful people in great shape sleeping with other people in great shape, partying and celebrating, and finally letting loose after what were probably years of tough training and strict diets.

The Olympic motto of "Swifter, Higher, Stronger" doesn't just apply to the competition. When they say the Olympics are about bridging international gaps and forging new and better world understandings, I guess this is part of what they were talking about. It wasn't unusual to see a sprinter from Africa leaving a room together with a discus thrower from Finland. I saw tall volleyball players leaving rooms with short weight lifters.

Imagine being an athletic person with a tremendous body who just achieved a lifetime goal. Imagine having four or five days to celebrate that achievement. Imagine being surrounded by other athletic people with the same tremendous bodies who have just achieved many of the same goals. And imagine all of you being thousands of miles from home and incredibly horny.

Sex in the Olympic Village is actually another three-letter word: Duh.

I do not kiss and tell about such things, but I will mention someone who I did not kiss during those days. A couple of times in the Village, I saw Clarissa Chun, who had finished fifth. Not once did we say a word to each other. We were once so close and now, at the height of our careers, we couldn't even speak. It was so sad. I hope someday we can be friends, because, among the women in my life, I may have never had a better friend.

At the end of the Olympics I flew home, although I quickly realized I might never again go home, as first I flew to Los Angeles, then New York, then Tokyo, then Chicago, then, finally, Phoenix.

Coach, all the way. Middle seats, all the way. From superstar back to slumdog, that was me.

My first stop was in Los Angeles for the *Tonight Show*. Somehow, I had made the cut and they had asked me to come onto the show. And somehow, it was going to be even better than expected, because they were flying in my mother from Colorado Springs and she was going to join me on the set. Believe it or not, it would have been the first time we'd seen each other since I had won the gold medal.

At least, I thought so, until about an hour before the show, when I was told that she was sick and couldn't leave the hotel. And I was furious. I was angry at her for not putting out the effort to come see me, and I was angry at the *Tonight Show* people for leading me on, and, more than anything, I was angry at myself for showing everyone how much I cared. I mean, how many other Olympic gold medalists are fighting off tears when they are told their mother is not coming onto a television show to see them?

"This sucks!" I said.

"Get out there and do your best anyway," said Tracy, trying to comfort me.

"I'm calling her!" I said.

"I wouldn't do that," said Tracy.

I didn't care. I called her, and that is when I nearly started crying, as I pleaded with her to get out of bed and join me in my moment.

"Mama, I haven't seen you in weeks, we have to celebrate this together, you are so close, I need you, I need you now!" I said.

"No, no," she kept saying. "I just can't."

So I sighed and took Tracy's advice and took the stage at my Cejudo best. I smiled and joked and bounced around that chair like everybody's favorite Mexican mascot. The crowd was cheering, Jay was laughing, and then I went in for the kill.

I told the Chicken Suit Story.

I put it in capital letters because it has since become sort of a symbol of my life. I have not written about it until now because, hey, I had to save some good stuff for last, didn't I?

Anyway, I was a freshman in high school, and I was trying to raise money for a trip to Chicago. There was an important junior wrestling tournament there. I had one day to raise the funds. Some guy heard me talking about it at church and offered me a job at his restaurant. A Mexican restaurant that specialized in chicken. Maybe you can see where this is going.

So I go over to his place after church, and I walk inside expecting to wash dishes or mop floors, but instead he hands me this rubber chicken suit, tells me to put it on, and pushes me back toward the door.

"Go outside, on the street, and get people to come into my restaurant," he said.

"Um, okay," I said.

So for two hours, in Arizona 115-degree temperatures, wearing a rubber chicken suit, I danced on the streets of Phoenix. I did cartwheels. I did spins. I did the salsa. I did the merengue. I even did the freaking moonwalk, anything to attract cars and to get them to pull into the parking lot and go to the restaurant. When I was finally nearing either asphyxiation or stroke, I walked inside for a drink of water.

"Two hours is enough for one day; you are done," said the boss as I pulled off my suit.

"Thanks. Can I get paid now?" I said.

"Sure," he said, walking over to cash register and pulling out one bill.

A ten-dollar bill.

For nearly killing myself, I was paid five bucks an hour, but the story sadly doesn't end there. I was so exhausted that I summoned a taxi to take me home, and at the end of the car ride when I arrived home and saw the fare, I became aware of the real crime of that afternoon.

I had been paid ten dollars, but the fare was twelve dollars.

Everybody laughs when I tell that story, so I keep telling it. And everyone laughed on Leno when I told it. But then, suddenly, everyone got quiet. It was the end of my appearance, and I figured that meant it was time to leave, when Leno told me he had a surprise for me.

And then there she was, coming out from behind that thick stage curtain, Nelly Rico, my mother.

Those bastards. Those beauties. The show's producers had fooled me, but never in my life was I happier to be the sucker, and I ran into my mother's arms and hugged her for the first time since I left for Beijing. You can probably guess what she said.

"This medal can make you great," she whispered, almost talking into the medal itself. "Or this medal can kill you."

By then, I had pretty much stopped listening to that warning. It was all great, and why would it ever change?

One moment Leno, the funniest guy on television. The next moment Oprah Winfrey, the hottest woman on television. I'm serious. On one of my stops before returning to Phoenix, I appeared in Chicago on the Oprah show with many other U.S. Olympic gold medalists. I didn't actually speak on the show—

they only showed a short video on my life—but I did get to shake her hand and talk to her, and I can only say one thing.

She really is hot. You can feel Oprah's power and strength in those hands. I know I'm probably not her type and too young, but, man, readers should know that men find confidence and influence very attractive, and she certainly had both.

Chicago was also a place where I later had the pleasure of honoring Art Martori, the founder of the Phoenix-based Sunkist Kids Wrestling Club, when he was inducted into the National Italian American Sports Hall of Fame. I haven't written about Mr. Martori before now because he likes to stay in the background, but while training for the Olympics I traveled to many meets as part of his club, and on his dime, and I could not have won a gold medal without him. I hope he will forgive me for writing even this little bit about him, but my story would not be complete without a mention of him.

My two other stops before returning home included one stop in New Jersey to meet one of the generous donors who had helped fund my sixty-five-thousand-dollar Olympic award check, the kind of money the USOC understandably can't pay to "amateur" athletes . . . And I traveled all the way to Japan for another stop in Tokyo to appear on an embarrassing show that I endured because it involved extra money.

It was a Japanese game show called *Sasuke*, or *Ninja Warrior*. It is basically a televised obstacle course that is supposed to test your toughness. They called me because they wanted to test my sportsmanship and agility. They wanted me to compete in this obstacle course against Tomihiro Matsunaga, the Japanese wrestler who I had defeated in the gold-medal match.

I was paid ten thousand dollars to face Matsunaga in the final round of the show, only he had been practicing, and I had just gotten off the plane and was pretty whacked out and jet-lagged. It was very awkward in the beginning, standing next to the guy whose ass I had kicked, standing in front of Japanese fans who clearly didn't like me. I tried to inspire myself by chanting, "U-S-A! U-S-A!" It sounds cool on television, but, you know, it never much works in real life.

It was awkward, and then it was just ugly, as I immediately stumbled and fell into a bunch of mud while Matsunaga was racing around the course. I lost badly. I got filthy, and everyone was laughing at me. But later that night in a Tokyo bar, ten thousand dollars richer, I celebrated like a champ.

I know some Olympic champions are careful about their endorsements and appearances, but not me. I knew that I may never have this opportunity again. If I was ever going to spread my message of hard work and hope and a belief in the greatness of America, if I was ever going to tell my story, it would have to be now or never. You want me at a grade school? I'm there. You want me in a boardroom? I'm there.

You want me on *Dancing with the Stars*? Actually, they just wanted to interview me for a spot on the show, so I drove to Los Angeles and met with their people. I thought I would be perfect. Wrestlers have the best hips of any athletes in the world. Wrestlers have the quickest contortions, the smoothest moves, and the strongest reflexes. How could they turn me down?

Actually, they never officially turned me down. They told me they would call me. And I'm still waiting for that call. Meanwhile, it seems like another Beijing Olympian, Shawn Johnson, not only stole my spot, but stole my victory. Just kidding. But I do love to dance, and I'll dance anywhere, from a Phoenix schoolyard filled with kids to a club in Las Vegas. Why haven't I mentioned this before now? Before August of 2008, there was never much reason to dance. I was too busy training to take time out to tango.

At last, a couple of weeks after the Games, I felt like dancing when I finally landed at my home in Phoenix, finally back among my people, old men coming out of little houses with barred windows to hug me, young guys coming out of the backs of restaurants to wipe their hands and shake mine, old women pressing packs of fresh tamales into my hands. While I talked to everyone as I drove around my old neighborhoods—remember, I lived in about a dozen apartments there—I gave official speeches at my old Maryvale High and a local Mexican restaurant where they used to give me free food. It was truly a trip through my past, both inspiring and scary.

Talk about a trip through my past.

At Maryvale, I felt like Elvis, with everyone cheering and teachers who had barely noticed me when I was a student there suddenly wanting my autograph and to give me a hug. While I looked mostly at the kids in the seats in front of me, I raised my voice so I could be heard in the back, by the kids who went unnoticed, either by design or not. They, too, were my people.

Then I spoke at a local Mexican restaurant that was run by the father of a former wrestling buddy. We used to come here for free food after practice, so it was only fair that I visit since I'm a big eater. Although in connecting with the unchanged part of my past, it was the first time I realized that I was not completely the same, that even though things like this restaurant were the same, I had changed in big ways. Some things still stayed the same, though, because, throughout my speech in front of hundreds of old friends, all I could think was, damn, there are a bunch of drunk Mexicans here and somebody is going to get in a fight.

Yeah, I was sometimes still uncomfortable in my own home, but I loved it just the same, at least the parts of it that still spoke to me.

Then there were the parts of it that still rejected me. It was sadly not a surprise when, while driving around Phoenix, I turned on talk radio in my car to hear hosts and listeners complaining about my mother. Yes, my mother.

"Deport her," said one.

"She should be back in Mexico where she belongs," said another.

"I don't care if her son is a gold medalist; she's a criminal," said someone else.

At one point, I pulled into a Circle K parking lot, put the car in park, turned the car off, and banged the steering wheel a couple of times in anger. I had just won a gold medal for their country and they wanted to kick out my mother?

News flash, people: She has a green card. She is allowed to work here like you or me. And now, thanks to my gold medal, I was able to pull some bureaucratic strings and help her acquire a Mexican passport, so she can travel like you or me.

Yes, she came here illegally, but wouldn't you? In fact, maybe you did, and why wouldn't everybody want to come here? It's the greatest country in the world. It allows people to be whatever they want to be. Who can blame her for coming here? And then she does a damn good job raising a family against all odds and producing a kid who represents this country with a gold medal and suddenly she doesn't belong? I wanted to pile-drive those talk-show hosts and their bigoted listeners. I want to scream to the people of Phoenix that I'm not Mexican, I'm not Mexican-American, I'm just American.

Fortunately, most people see me that way. Mostly, this gold medal has turned me into something that has no race or color or nationality. I'm just an American champion. Mine was simply an American victory. Not only for the folks in South Central Los Angeles or downtown Las Cruces or the Phoenix barrio or the Colorado Springs suburbs. An American victory for all of us.

But some people still don't get it. Some people still see my gold medal not as a trophy, but a target. Since winning the medal, I've been constantly challenged in bars. People just walking up wanting to fight me, wanting to tell their friends that they kicked the ass of an Olympic wrestling champion.

Within a couple of months of returning home, I was in two brawls and didn't start either one. The first one was in Phoenix. A guy pushed me as I was standing next to the bar and ten of my buddies jumped him and that was the end of that. The second one, in Colorado Springs, was messier. Once again, some guys surrounded me at the bar, chanting about how I was a pussy champion, and then my brother Alonzo jumped in, only this time he got pounded, so I had to start throwing the punches to protect him.

It was at this point that I suddenly thought I could be an Olympic boxer. I mean, man, I had no idea how much weight I packed into each of my punches. Guys were flying around like in a video game. I'm just a little guy, so fools were lining up to take me down, but nobody did; it was crazy. Then the police showed up, and saw one of those poor guys on the ground, and I ran out with Alonzo following me. I ran faster, and they caught him. I feel bad because he ended up spending the night in jail, but he was released the next morning and nothing ever happened. It was self-defense, and the cops knew it.

Since those times, I have avoided bars, especially my two old haunts. I have spent most of my time flying around giving speeches, basing them on three words that having nothing to do with partying.

Dream. Sacrifice. Victory. I talk about how, with anything in life, you must dream big and sacrifice hard before you can truly enjoy victory. I talk about no excuses, about how I was from a home where I grew up with little food, thin shelter, and no father, and you know what? Nobody ever let me use it as an excuse. Nobody ever let me be the victim. Don't be the victim. Attack life before it attacks you. If I can make it, hell, anybody can make it.

And then again, sometimes I talk about dolls.

I was in Washington, D.C., making the rounds of visits with some other Olympic champions on a trip that seemed doomed for disaster before it even started. I screwed up on my flight, landed late, and took a cab to the wrong hotel, where I was welcomed with a funny look, and soon I learned why.

I was at the hotel for the Paralympians, the disabled Olympians. The other Olympians were somewhere else. It was too late to change, so I spent the entire trip hanging out with true Olympic heroes, athletes in wheelchairs, incredibly strong athletes with incredibly strong wills.

One day we were at Walter Reed Hospital when organizers rushed up to me and asked if I could speak to a bunch of military dignitaries. The softball star Jennie Finch was supposed to talk, but for some reason she wasn't there.

I agreed, but then I thought, What could I possibly say? I looked out at an audience filled with commanders and lieutenants and thought, Whoa, I'm just a wrestler.

Then it hit me. Yeah, okay, I'm just a wrestler, and that's going to have to be enough.

So I talked about G.I. Joe. I told them that growing up in a house with no toys, nothing was as valuable as my borrowed G.I. Joe. I talked about how I made that doll do amazing things, how I would have him protect other dolls, protect my sliver of bed, even protect my scant helping of beans and rice. Growing up, G.I. Joe stood watch over my life despite his small size and limited strength.

I told these guys that, in winning a gold medal, I was simply following in his footsteps, and I was proud to use the military as my role model, and everyone was laughing. Then, soon, everyone was standing, a huge ovation that warmed my heart and made me think that maybe I could be a public speaker one day. I may need to start bringing along a G.I. Joe as a prop. But it has to be the one with the kung-fu grip because that's the one that I had.

I have pretty much attacked my post-Olympic experience like I attacked my wrestling and training. If you want me, you're gonna get all of me, even the shirt off my back, sometimes literally. I was in Iran as a wrestling ambassador during an international meet several months after the Olympics, and was stunned that all these so-called political enemies were hugging me and holding my hand like a girlfriend and congratulating me on my victory. Wrestling is a really big deal there. But, so, too, is an appreciation for struggle, and I was honored that they showed me so much of their genuine appreciation. In return, I gave them what they wanted. I gave them my shirt, my singlet, my socks, my shoes, souvenirs for everyone. In return, they would give me boxes of pistachios. I remember once walking out of an Iranian arena wearing my underwear, but carrying two boxes of nuts, and holding hands with an aging, heavyset Iranian man. That's the custom there. I thought to myself, Thank goodness the paparazzi don't have visas to see me now.

Sometimes I get nuts. Other times I get more gold.

This happened after I spoke at a Special Olympics banquet. A developmentally disabled girl came up to me and told me that my story had touched her life, which brought a lump to my throat. Then she said she was also a gold medal winner in her Special Olympic event, and wanted to know if I would exchange gold medals with her.

"I'm sorry. I can't. My mother would kill me," I told her.

"That's okay," she said with a sigh.

Then she pulled out her gold medal and put it around my neck.

"You know what?" she said. "You can just have mine anyway."

Then she spun around and disappeared through the crowd, many of whom looked at me funny when I later started crying.

Today I keep that gold medal in a drawer next to mine, and I carry it with me for every appearance, then pull both medals out, and ask everyone to guess which medal means more.

They always guess wrong.

What a wonderful life I lead now, touching and being touched by all these wonderful people, using my medal to evolve and grow while trying never to forget my roots.

I bought a used Mercedes, sixty thousand miles, even though

I still really don't know how to drive it. And I still live in an apartment owned by Tracy, and that apartment still just has one bedroom. I have spent little money on my own clothes, preferring to hang out in sweatshirts and jeans still.

Sometimes, when I get frustrated during all my travels, I will go into the airplane bathroom and shadowbox. Other times, I will find a church and a Bible study, like the one in Phoenix where the leaders asked me to bring in my gold medal. When I did, one of the teachers saw it and shook his head.

"You need to hold on to that loosely, Henry," he said.

"Why?" I asked.

"Because you ain't taking it to heaven," he said.

I try to remember that as I spread my message. I try to remember that it is not the medal's embrace that will ultimately save me, but the embrace of everyone I can touch and inspire with it.

While I never made much money from wrestling—the average champion gets a stipend of under twenty thousand dollars a year—I have been able to make some money in endorsements, in both Spanish and English, although my eyes have been opened about how some companies differentiate.

I remember negotiating with an athletic apparel outfit about a deal, and suddenly they asked me about a criminal record, asked me if I had been in jail, asked me about drugs, asked me about friends, asked me a bunch of questions that led to one conclusion.

They didn't trust me, and I didn't know why, until Tracy Greiff figured it out.

"Wait a minute," he told them. "Would you ask the same questions of Rulon Gardner?"

He was referring to the giant white wrestling champion.

And course they said they would ask him the same questions. But of course they would not.

This one incident did not dissuade or disillusion me, though. Having spent nearly a year traveling the land with a piece of its heart hanging around my neck, I have become convinced that the greatest thing about this country is its ability to look beyond color and creed and only see American. I am in love with the awesome chances given to each of those Americans, a chance that even a poor kid with undocumented parents can seize and twist and pull and pin into the fulfillment of a dream.

Only in America could my outsized dreams be realized, even if that realization takes fifteen years and lasts just about four quick minutes.

It was two days after I won the gold medal. My muscles were aching for some steam, so Tracy Greiff and I ducked into his Beijing hotel sauna. We were sitting in our towels in his hotel sauna when he popped the question.

"So what now?" he said

"What now?" I said.

"Yeah, like, what are your next plans for wrestling?" he said.

I paused. I had been thinking about this from the moment the gold-medal referee raised my hand.

I had been thinking about the years of pain, thinking about the mountains of sacrifice, thinking about the perfect ending, wondering how it could be any better, wondering if my message would get diluted if the ending was eventually something worse.

"Well, I've thought about it," I told Tracy.

"And?" he said.

"I quit," I said. "I'm done."

Just like that, my unlikely dreams having been fulfilled, I decided to devote my life to helping others chase their own.

Some will say that, at age twenty-one, I decided to quit too soon. Others will hopefully agree that for the sake of spreading this incredible gift, I am quitting just in time. In any case, I'm reserving the right to change my mind, particularly in light of USA Wrestling's pledge to pay Olympic champions $250,000 each in 2012. I'm stubborn, but I'm not dumb.

Whatever happens, if you see me in your town someday, stop by and say hello and join me in celebrating the opportunities afforded us by the greatest country on earth.

An American victory deserves an American ending.

Sweet land of liberty, of thee I will sing.

ACKNOWLEDGMENTS

As a team, the authors would like to thank Craig Sesker and Gary Abbott of USA Wrestling, without whose headlocks and pile drivers this book would be impossible. We would like to thank Tracy Greiff, whose kind and generous actions provided the seeds for this story. We would like to thank all those who spent the time to tell the real tale of the American Victory, including Henry's official family and his wrestling family, from Gloria Cejudo to Angel Cejudo, from Frank Saenz to Terry Brands. Finally, we would also like to thank Laura Perciasepe, whose patience gave this book breadth and whose editing gave it life.

I would like to thank my family, my friends, and my supporters. My family: Barbara, Alonzo, Gloria, George, Angel, Christina, and the one and only, the terminator, my mother, Nelly Rico. I'd also like to thank Tracy Greiff, Eric Albaracin and the Hurtado family. At USA Wrestling, I would like to thank Rich Bender, Doc Bennett, Craig Sesker, Gary Abbott. I'd also like to thank the United States Olympic Committee, including Bill and Jim Scherr. I would like to thank wrestling's greatest supporters Art Martori, Brian Giffin, Dave Berry, Mike Novogratz, Steve Silver, John Bardis, Jeff Levitetz, and Ken Honig. And for the book, I'd like to thank Laura Perciasepe, Bill Plaschke, Lydia Wills, Ray Garcia and everyone at Penguin. For my coaches, I'd like to thank Terry Brands, Kevin Jackson, Doc Bennett (again), Frank Saenz, Richard Fimbres, Brian Davis, Matt Brickell, and Sergei Beloglazov. And I want to thank the people that put me together and gave me a great smile, Dr. Glauser, Dr. Sullavan, and Dr. Mark B. Burdorf. The people who sponsored me: Brute, Adidas, Tom Scully, Jeff Bowyer, the Zero Scale, Greg Nunley, Rich Creps and Don. The people who supported me and have been a big influence on me: Cole Kelly, Joe Uva, Kenny Ortega, Jerry Colangelo, Mike Sotello, Mike Wang, Noel Thompson, Otto Padron, and my new best friends, Travis and Kathy Holcombe. And I'd like to thank the beautiful twins, Lulu and Lala.

I'd also like to thank Aaron Polansky, Aaron Simpson, Adam Desabado, Albert Torres, Aldo Mesa, Alex Coronado, Al Fuentes, Andy Patman, Andy Rovat, Anthony Fimbres, Anthony Robles, Arlene Limas, Brian Davis, Ben Askren, Ben Kar, Bill McFarlane, Blanca Torres, Bob Barson, Bobby Douglas, Bobby Lashley, Brandon Hut, Breanne Vovar, Brian Keck, Brian Stith, Bryce Hassemen, Cain Velasquez, Charlie Huber, Chrae Pasqua, Chris Greenman, Chris Simeck, Chuchi, Crazy Chuck Liddell, Cisco, Conine family, Craig Martin, Darrell Miller, Daniel Cormier, Danielle Hurtado, Danny Alcorse, Dan Davine, Danny Keffler,

Danny Perru, Darello Barela, Dave Esposito, David Garcia, David Preciado, Dean Morrison, Derrick Peperas, Desiree, Diamond, Diane Simpson, Dr. Carrasco, Dr. Hernandez, Duane Venken, Eddie Albarracin, Eli Arismendez, Emmett Blahnik, Ernesto Gastelum, Filipe Corral, Franky Sanchez, Harry (USA Wrestling), Hector Gomez, Hector Placencia, Hudson Collins, Ivan Ivanoff, Jay Robinson, Jay Allen, JD, Jamie McNab, Jake Diechtler, Jake Hurbert, Javier Mendez, Jenny Quezada, Jeremy Wilson, Jesse Abarca, Jessica Love, Jim Murphy, Jimmy Clips, Joe Hesket, Joey Law, Joe Sotello, John Mora, John Davis, Josh Churrella, Josh Corona, Juan Garcia, Juan Mora, Junior Cortez, Justin Robles, Katherine Hurtado, Kathleen Mascarenas, Kenny Lester, Kira Sreeloan, Kyle Seminara, Larry Langowski, Larry Slater, Lee Fulhart, Leo Martinez, Luis Olivares, Luis Vendejas, Manny Molina, Marco Toledo, Miguel Freas, Mo Law, Nick Lopez, Niko Salazar, Norm Frauenheim, Pablo Roqueta, Paula Lopez, Ramon Robles, Randi Miller, Randy George, Randy Gordon, Randy Lewis, Raquel Albaraccin, Raul Jaimes, Ray Arvizu, Ray Borrego, Reader's Digest, Ricardo Liborio, Rey Misterio, Robert Luera, Ron Groves, Rodney Stafford, Rusty Davie, Ryan Hockensmith, Ryan Lockwood, Sanaz, Scott Peters, Shannon Slack, Sean Bormet, Steve Fraser, Steve Lawson, TC Danzler, Tara Hitchcock, Tommy Rowlands, Tommy Marquez, Townsend Saunders, Urijah Faber, Vanessa Oswalt, Vicente Varela, Victor Guerrero, Vicente Cordero, Viola Cruz, Whitney Conder, Z Enrique, Z Enrique's family, and Zev Miller.

Bill Plaschke would like to personally thank his parents, Grover and Mary Plaschke, for always being there, always coaching, always cheering, particularly when his shoulders were on the

Acknowledgments ★

mat, He would also like to thank his children—T-Berry, Boy-Boy and M.C.—for their constant hugs and endless patience. Thanks to his siblings Brad, Beth and Bob, for always picking up the phone even when Bill sometimes had a cauliflower ear. Thanks to Danielle English for her constant and unconditional support, not to mention her giggles. If it wasn't for Kevin Baxter grabbing Bill out of a cool pressroom on a steamy afternoon in Beijing and dragging him to a weird wrestling match, this book would have never happened, so thanks to Kevin. Finally, thanks to manager Michael Price for giving him the advice to start the book, *Los Angeles Times* boss Randy Harvey for giving him the time to write it, and Gene Wojciechowski for giving him the inspiration to finish it.

ABOUT THE AUTHORS

Henry Cejudo is a freestyle wrestler who won a gold medal in the 2008 Beijing Olympics. At twenty-one years old, he was the youngest American ever to have won an Olympic wrestling gold medal. Henry was born in Los Angeles, and lives in Phoenix, Arizona, and Colorado Springs, Colorado.

Bill Plaschke has been named the Associated Press Sports Columnist of the Year four times. He has been a sports columnist for the *Los Angeles Times* since 1996 and is a regular panelist on ESPN'S *Around the Horn*. He has been nominated for a Pulitzer Prize and his work has been featured frequently in *The Best American Sports Writing*.